How To
Start And Operate
A Luxury
Pet Boarding Kennel For
Cats

A Pet Oriented, Home Based, Career Change Or Retirement Business Opportunity.

Joseph Garvey

Published By
Garvey Associates

About The Author

After graduation from High School, Joe Garvey hoped for a future as a major league baseball player. One workout at a major league tryout camp demonstrated pro ball would not be his day job.

On completing college, he joined his father-in-law's advertising business, subsequently working for a number of major marketing and advertising firms where he managed multimillion dollar campaigns for national and international companies manufacturing both consumer and business products.

Founding his own firm in 1982, Garvey dedicated most of his time to his favorite side of the business, serving as Creative Director, where he created and wrote advertising campaigns in addition to serving as CEO.

On semi-retiring in 1991, Joe and his wife Carol began working with a specialized foster care program for disadvantaged children. This effort evolved into a passion in which they are still involved, assisting children in moving on to a better life. During this period they also founded a luxury Bed & Breakfast for cats to care for cats when pet owners had to be absent from home (www.pamperedcats.com)

Garvey's stories are drawn from the experiences caring for the children and pets they have loved and cared for over the years. His first book, "Starting and Operating A Luxury Bed & Breakfast For Cats" shares a wealth of information of great value to anybody interested in starting or reading about starting such a business. The book also has a number of fascinating stories about cats.

Additional stories will be drawn from a treasure trove of background material provided by Carol's great aunt's periodical collection, a barnful of magazines uncovered after her death dating back to the Civil War.

Joseph Garvey lives on the shore of Massachusetts Bay just a short drive from Cape Cod.

ISBN-13: 978-1-944771-00-3
Printed In the United States of America

INTRODUCTION

Life, as they say, is a journey, and the roots of the road traveled often originate in the distant past. In our case, my wife Carol and I would definitely be in a far different place were it not for a conversation overheard on a sand dune overlooking Cape Cod Bay in the early 1900s.

The dunes were located in Plymouth, Massachusetts, America's hometown. The conversation indicated the participants were contemplating building a cottage on the site. Although my wife's great grandfather owned the land, "squatters" were a problem at the time, and great-grandfather decided to get busy building his own cottage on the dune to forestall any problems. It would be far easier to build on the location himself than to try to get the squatters removed. The cottage he ultimately built would become the anchor of the family's presence on the beach for generations to come.

When my wife Carol and I were dating in the late 50s, we spent a lot of time during the summers at Whitehorse Beach, where the cottage is located. During those visits, Carol had pointed out a nearby house that held great fascination for her. It was a large, rambling New England farmhouse with spacious front porch, attractive landscaping, and a view overlooking two immaculately kept Cranberry bogs. As the years passed the home fell into serious disrepair.

By 1976 it was vacant and completely boarded up. Out of curiosity we stopped by one day, and walking to the rear of the lot, saw one of the window panels had been removed. Local kids had broken in and were using the house as a party pad. After getting a peek inside I knew Carol was not going to be denied a tour of the house. She had talked to a local broker who had keys but told her he could not sell the home because of financial issues the bank had with the property. Since he was a nice guy, however, and probably felt he could sell us something else, he finally agreed to take us over for a quick tour.

The mess in the house was beyond belief. Suffice it to say that in addition to the clutter there was a complete lack of amenities. All the interior doors were painted a deathly dark burgundy color. The so-called "kitchen" featured a range with a slide-in burner-shelf located in what looked like a 4' x 8' cubby hole. The living room presented with a partially collapsed suspended ceiling, two awkwardly positioned support posts in the middle of the room, and a number of those deathly doors. Upstairs we found five bedrooms, the door to each featuring a brass identification number and dead bolt lock. The dead bolts, interestingly, could only be operated from the hallway side of the door. We later found out the property had been used as a halfway house for drug and alcohol abuse clients.

The place seemed outright scary to me and I was ready to leave when I heard Carol murmer,

"This house has great bones."

I should have known then and there this money pit was destined to play a role in my life. Little did I know exactly how large that role would be. We attempted to talk to the president of the bank, but he wouldn't even discuss selling the property. The bank President told us the home would be auctioned in October, since they would probably be able to get the best price possible at that time of the year.

As October approached Carol tentatively brought up the subject once again.

"It might be fun to go to a real estate auction. We've never done that before. We can check on the cottage while we're down there, go out to lunch, you know, we'll make it a nice relaxing day. "

Auction day finally arrived. It was a warm, sunny, Indian Summer day with a light sea breeze that carried an invigorating salt air scent in from the shoreline located a few hundred yards away. At 10:00 am, the appointed time for the auction, we were the only ones present besides the bank president and auctioneer. The two of them stalled as long as they could, obviously hoping for more potential bidders to arrive, but were finally forced by the clock to proceed.

As the auctioneer made his final preparations the bank president walked over and asked if we were going to bid. I told him we had only come out of curiosity to see what would happen. He advised us, almost apologetically, the law required the bank to bid at least the amount of the mortgage on the property, and added that under current circumstances he would bid the mortgage amount. All we had to do was bid ten dollars more. As he started to walk away he paused, turned back toward us and muttered we could bid five dollars more, or even a dollar and the house was ours.

As the auctioneer started his chant we feared a late arrival with the money to win the auction might show, but that did not happen. The banker made his formal bid and I decided to be a big spender, bidding $10 more than the bank – some $32K and change. The auctioneer declared the property sold and the bank president came over to us, accepted my thousand dollar check, and placed a set of keys in my hand with the admonition the property was ours to protect from that point on and we would hear shortly from the bank about a closing date.

And that is how we came to live at the home that would one day become a Luxury Bed and Breakfast for kitties.

In the intervening years, before we started the B&B, that big old home served as an ideal place to raise our four children. For a number of years I ran my own advertising business out of the portion of the house eventually converted into our luxury kitty bed-and-breakfast. Ultimately, in 1997, Pampered Cats was born, and we were on the road to a very unusual innkeeping career.

CAT NAPS

From time to time we will take a break from the business side of feline inn keeping for a "Catnap." Catnaps are stories of life in the "cat house" in which we share the humor, trials, and joys that are an integral part of being an innkeeping host to the wonderful world of felines.

PREFACE

This book lays out how we started our own luxury boarding kennel, also often called a pet hotel or cat Bed and Breakfast, and describes each stage of the journey. Creating such a business is obviously within the reach of any cat-loving enthusiast and offers a great opportunity for individuals seeking to make a career change or establish a home based business to meet retirement or work from home goals.

Although we have always had cats of our own, we had no experience running an animal care business before we started our business. For nineteen years we have run a successful business started with an investment of less than $5,000. (I did build all our condos myself and really enjoyed the process). Sales have increased every year since we started and weathered the recent recession quite nicely. There is a growing need for the services Bed & Breakfast Hotels for cats provide, and well planned facilities are experiencing strong demand. You will also find that cat owners, in general, are the nicest people you will ever want to work with.

If you are looking for an opportunity to work for yourself, escape commuting, eliminate other people telling you what to do, and possibly worrying about being laid off, this may be the business opportunity you are looking for.

Our objective in this book is to give you an overview of all aspects of starting and operating a kitty B&B. We'll get started by taking a look at how our own kitty B&B got off the ground.

Table of Contents

CHAPTER 5

CHAPTER 6

CHAPTER 7

CHAPTER 8

CHAPTER 9

CHAPTER 1

OVERVIEW

When we decided to go away to Maine for a long weekend we never dreamed a chain of events was being initiated that would result in our establishing a luxury "Bed & Breakfast" for cats.

For years we had college age and working children around to care for our cats when we were away. Shortly after our youngest son married and moved out, we were grounded as we had no one to care for the cats. We had wanted to go away to Maine for a long weekend for quite some time, but with no one to look after our kitties we had to go out and tour boarding kennels. That's when we began to realize finding our pampered kitties a place to stay that was just like home was not going to be easy. The cages at many places we visited were extremely small. In a few establishments dogs were located near and sometimes right across the aisle from the cats. We knew our cats were going to be totally freaked out.

One day during our kitty boarding search Carol happened to open Yankee Magazine and saw the monthly House For Sale article. It featured a lady operating a cats-only boarding service out of her home in Maine. Each cat had a spacious enclosure big enough to house several cats from the same family when necessary. Each condo, as she called them, had a couple of sleeping shelves, cushions, toys and really big litter boxes. Because the service was operated out of her home, the animals were never left alone for hours at a time or overnight. The cats enjoyed premium food, had windows to look out, spent time outside their enclosure and enjoyed daily socialization time and brushing. The owner called her kennel a "Bed and Breakfast for Cats." After a tour, we found ourselves wishing there was something like it close to our home.

At that point everything jelled. We knew there was a need because there must be other people like us looking for a really special place to board their cat. Our big old empty nest home had a wing that would be perfect for the task. And that is the beginning of our story.

THE PSYCHOLOGY OF LUXURY PET BOARDING FACILITIES.

There has been a quantum shift going on over the past few years regarding people's attitudes towards their pets. Not long ago, pet care needs were met by kennels providing very basic, utilitarian facilities. Those kennels were patronized because there was nothing better available.

The increasing emotional needs of pet owners for higher class services began to be recognized by astute kennel operators. New kennels began featuring dramatic improvements to the boarding environment. Pet owners, most of whom believe their pet "is one of the family," responded favorably. Thus was born the era of luxury kennel facilities.

Today, luxury facilities providing day and overnight care for pets while owners travel or are on vacation are spreading fast. Services that would formerly have been joked about have now become standard fare. Doggy day care, luxury kitty B&Bs and hotels, taxi services to get animals to their appointments, dog and cat psychologists, acupuncture and more.

This all adds up to a great opportunity for entrepreneurs willing to go the extra mile and provide the services pet owners are looking for. Offer "homelike" amenities for pets so they are as comfortable as they would be at home and the world will beat a path to your door (if they know you exist). The one caveat is you must be willing to work energetically at marketing your business to create awareness in your market area.

THE EVOLUTION OF KITTY BED & BREAKFASTS AND HOTELS.

A few years ago most cat kennels featured a number of 2' x 2' wire cages crammed in a room with numerous cats. Infinitesimal sized litter boxes left even a small cat little room to turn around, and there was no room for a comfy bed from home, toys or anything else. Today, luxury hotels for cats offer large condos, outdoor views and many other amenities. Establishments range from large sized commercial sites to cozy, homey facilities such as our own (see our web site at www.pamperedcats.com).

Our B&B is located in a wing of our home, so the cats are always accompanied in the residence by the owners. This feature is highly prized by our customers, who do not want their kitties in a separate building, or worse still in a commercial building uninhabited at night and on weekends. As with human B&Bs, a big part of the customer experience arises out of the level of hospitality provided by the host. Human B&B owners are usually far more successful if they honestly like and enjoy working with people. The same applies to a feline B&B. You should like both cats and people.

The goal for any successful kitty B&B must be to offer all the amenities and services cat lovers seek. Our facility was designed with large windows in the boarding room featuring great outdoor views overlooking the cranberry bogs next door. Since the rooms face south, the windows permit plenty of natural light and sunshine to pour in, creating a warm, inviting atmosphere. Each guest is comfortably housed in a spacious, safe condo that is large enough to accommodate kitty's own bed, a really big litter box, toys and other personal effects from home. Each large condo at Pampered Cats measures about 3 x 4 x 8 foot high and has three separate levels so kitties have plenty of room to move around. Studio condos (3 x 3 x 4 foot) are ideal for senior cats with physical difficulties and for kittens. Kitty step stools are placed in the units for older cats so they can easily get from one level to another. The studio units are also safer for kittens, as kittens love to indulge in childish behavior, such as bouts of high-speed tail chasing that can lead to falls from the higher shelves in the large units. We don't want to take a chance on a kitten getting injured.

Cats are allowed free time out of their condo to roam around, play, check "what's happening" outside the windows and say hello to their neighbors if they want. The bottom line is to provide loving personal care, good food, cater to special diets, provide medications when needed and do whatever else it takes to make kitty comfortable. Each and every cat is treated like it was our own.

Being semi-retired, we're around home most of the time, so we frequently go into the cattery to interact with our guests during the day and evening. Before going to bed we also check in to make sure everything is OK and everyone is "tucked in" for the night. We feel better when we know all our kitties are doing just fine. That's what running a luxury B&B for cats is all about. And we have found our guests (most of them at least) and their owners richly reward us with appreciation for the special efforts made on their behalf.

The bottom line is our customers frequently tell us they are delighted to have found us and are happy to pay a reasonable price to know their pets are receiving loving care by people who own and love cats themselves.

CHAPTER 2

THE BUSINESS AND YOU

IS THIS A REAL BUSINESS OR AM I JUST DREAMING.

Luxury pet resorts that have evolved to meet the need for a better boarding alternative typically provide both daycare and longer term boarding for dogs. Since cats are relatively "low maintenance" pets, daycare is rarely needed. For owner absences of more than a day or two, cats can be cared for in highly attractive, home-like environments in many of these modern facilities.

The "luxury" segment of the pet care boarding industry has been growing by leaps and bounds. A simple Google search for "cat boarding" for example, will result in a listing of numerous facilities across the globe. The UK, you will find, is a hot bed of enthusiasm for the ultimate in kitty boarding facilities. You could also try a search on "cat boarding Plymouth ma" and you should get a listing including our site at www.pamperedcats.com, along with others. These searches will give you a feel for the scope of the industry at present.

Next, we would like to focus our discussion on presenting the particulars on the rapidly expanding Pet Care Industry sector of the U.S. economy. This information is of vital concern to anybody thinking of starting a pet care business.

Most of the statistics provided have been obtained from the American Pet Products Association (APPA) and we encourage you to visit their site (http://www.americanpetproducts.org/) and any others you come across that provide information on the industry.

According to APPA, the pet care industry has grown steadily from $17 billion in 1994 to $58 billion in 2014. As of the time of writing, expenditures in 2015 were projected to be $60 billion. Obviously, the pet care industry has been one of the most recession resistant areas of the economy. Following is a breakdown of expenditures for the last few years.

2010
Expenditures in Billions of Dollars on Pets

Food	18.76
Supplies; OTC Medicines	10.94
Vet Care	13.01
Live Animal Purchases	2.13
Pet Services: Grooming/Boarding	3.51

2011
Expenditures in Billions of Dollars on Pets

Food	19.53
Supplies; OTC Medicines	11.4
Vet Care	14.11
Live Animal Purchases	2.15
Pet Services: Grooming/Boarding	3.65

2012
Expenditures in Billions of Dollars on Pets

Food	20.64
Supplies; OTC Medicines	12.65
Vet Care	13.67
Live Animal Purchases	2.21
Pet Services: Grooming/Boarding	4.16

2013
Expenditures in Billions of Dollars on Pets

Food	21.26
Supplies; OTC Medicines	13.21
Vet Care	14.21
Live Animal Purchases	2.31
Pet Services: Grooming/Boarding	4.54

2014
Expenditures in Billions of Dollars on Pets

Food	22.26
Supplies; OTC Medicines	13.75
Vet Care	15.04
Live Animal Purchases	2.15
Pet Services: Grooming/Boarding	4.84

2015 (Projected)
Expenditures in Billions of Dollars on Pets

Food	23.04
Supplies; OTC Medicines	14.39
Vet Care	15.73
Live Animal Purchases	2.19
Pet Services: Grooming/Boarding	5.24

The foregoing statistics demonstrate the industry is in good health and an excellent segment of the economy in which to start a business in challenging times.

WHY A KITTY B&B OR HOTEL?

You might ask, "Why specialize in just cats? Why not board both dogs and cats?" The answer to this question depends on your objective and on how you plan to operate your business.

If your objective is to run a home-based business in a residential area, you may find that there are some formidable obstacles to be overcome in order to board dogs. Your municipality may not permit kenneling dogs in a non-commercial zone. You might be able to board whatever number of dogs the city or town allows individual homeowners to have, but that does not generate much in the way of revenue. We know a couple of people that do this for spare income, but that is all it will ever amount to.

If you can get approval for kenneling multiple dogs, you will need to have quite a bit of space in your building as well as land area outside. Dogs require a lot more room and personal attention than cats, making dog boarding far more labor intensive. This usually necessitates hiring staff if you want to board more than just a couple of dogs, and that can be expensive.

You will also find that many cat owners prefer to board their cats where there are no dogs, as the barking of unfamiliar dogs upsets their cats.

If your business plan requires working with limited space, such as a modified garage or outbuilding of some sort, or even an interior portion of your home similar to what we have done, cat boarding is a much less expensive endeavor on which to get started.

Two people, or even one person can easily run a typical mid-sized cat boarding facility. As previously mentioned, daily cleaning and other required activities at a cat B&B business can be completed in less than two hours a day even when boarding 20 or so cats.

Although dog boarding can generate more revenue, the additional expenses incurred will mean you have to grow the business to achieve financial equilibrium. At that point you may find you have circumvented your original plan of starting a small home operated business.

For comparison purposes, a cat bed and breakfast is easy to build and operate out of a relatively small space. Our operation has 18 units located in two rooms in a wing of our home containing approximately 300+ s/f. We could also easily add another 16 units in two adjacent rooms that occupy about 300 s/f.

A home-based B&B business, since all business activities take place at the home, enables a stay-at-home mom or dad to be at home for the kids and still earn an income at the same time. The home operation also fits in very nicely with situations where parents want to home school their children. We have provided specialized foster care for needy children while running the cat business for the past 20 years, and it has worked out very well. Running a business out of your home also has some tax advantages that a good accountant can point out to you.

One disadvantage of being on the property is some people may feel they have the right to drop by any time they like, but we find most people are considerate. To minimize this behavior, we carefully point out that we work by appointment only and ask people to make an appointment to avoid being inconvenienced by arriving only to find we are not in the office.

All in all though, we would have to say the advantages have outweighed the disadvantages for us over the past 18 years.

OPPORTUNITY CALLS - WORK FOR YOURSELF.

Today, good jobs are not easy to find even if you are an experienced professional. Opening your own business in a booming sector of the economy is one way to escape the current restrictive employment situation.

If you've never started a business, it can appear to be a daunting task. But once you get started things have a way of working out — especially when you have selected a healthy sector of the economy in which to operate.

Once my wife and I had decided we were going to go all-in and start this kitty B&B I spent three to four months, part time, designing and building the condos in which the kitties would reside. From time to time we would look at each other and what we were doing and say, "I sure hope someone is going to come to our party." But the research we had done always whispered in our ear that there were others that were successful at it and that we could be too. We found the success of the lady in Maine, who was operating in a relatively low population area, to be particularly encouraging

During the initial planning stages we had looked at building a garage attached to our home with an apartment on the top floor that we could rent. Our luxury cat emporium would be created in what would normally have been the garage area. At this point I am glad we scaled back and played it conservative. Our business has always done well, been very manageable, and is not saddled with a lot of overhead. Our total cost, including materials, was under $5,000.

It is important if you are going to start a home based business that you enjoy being around home. Some people enjoy this lifestyle and some do not. If you are not a "homebody" sort of person, a home-based business may not be a good choice for you.

Working from home, however, does have many advantages - like making it possible for one parent to be around home for the children and still be producing an income. People that operate a kitty B&B, such as ourselves, often run more than one business from home. I have performed consulting and writing projects, written this book and created and produced websites at the same time we have been running the cat business. All these activities have dovetailed together quite nicely.

Another advantage is eliminating the wasted time and expense of commuting to the city – a 50 mile trip each way. For us, when you consider the cost of gasoline, automobile maintenance, clothing and other expenses, working from home has some considerable advantages.

If you love animals, you should find working with cats very rewarding. Most of the cats will favor you with love and affection once they get to know you (some won't, but just humor them). And when you take good care of your customers' pets, you will find them very appreciative and loyal to your business. Actually, the cat owners we have met during our time boarding cats are the nicest group of people I have ever had the privilege of working with. Owners are effusively thankful for the care we give to their little friends. People bring us gifts purchased on their trips that range from flowers and boxes of French chocolates to salt-water taffy from Atlantic City and more. Many of the kitties regularly send us holiday cards. These wonderful people lavish us with appreciation for the care and love we give their cherished pets.

Above all, you will find great satisfaction in building and operating a business that is respected in the community at large and with the animal care professionals you will come in contact with who can be a considerable influence on your future success.

WHAT DOES A TYPICAL DAY IN THE KITTY B&B LOOK LIKE?

Since my wife and I own and operate the B&B and have no employees, we are involved in every aspect of the operation.

Typically, our day starts about 8:00 am with cleaning and feeding. Each unit is cared for one at a time, so only one cat (or two or three if they are from the same family and in the same unit) are out of their condo at any given time. Each unit is cleaned and vacuumed and wiped down with disinfectant. Litter boxes are scooped, dry food dishes refilled, and water bowls cleaned and resupplied. Wet food is served in disposable paper food trays and then the guest goes back into their unit as we move on to take care of the next "room." If any cats require medication, these are administered as required along with their breakfast. Some cats also have to receive medications in the evening along with their dinner meal.

After cleaning and feeding activities are completed, we spend a few minutes double-checking on reservations and arrivals and departures scheduled for the day. These appointments are normally arranged between 9:00 – 10:00 am or 4:00 – 5:00 pm to leave the middle portion of the day free. Since cats do not require frequent attention, as dogs do, we have more freedom than if we were boarding dogs. Thankfully, we do not have to "walk" kitty to "take care of business."

ONE SPECIFIC DAY

My wife Carol and I have provided therapeutic foster care for children-in-need for more than twenty years. This makes our daily schedule similar to parents forty years younger than we are. One recent day at the kitty B&B looked something like this.

6:30 AM

Joe and Carol get up, get dressed and Joe heads down to start breakfast for the kids as Carol calls, "School day, time to get up."

7:15 AM

Julia and Mel grogg over their cereal while Joe and Carol grab a quick breakfast.

7:45 AM

It's a sunny day in October and in the good weather we often sit on the front porch and chat with the girls while we wait for Julia's bus. It arrives and Julia climbs aboard and is off to school. Joe now heads to the boarding room to get started on morning chores.

8:15 AM

Joe is in full swing tending to our feline visitors. Mel hollers in the window from the front porch, "Joe, my bus is coming, bye," and off she goes to kindergarten. The feeding and cleaning activities this morning only takes about 40 minutes to complete, as most of the kitties were well behaved last night.

9:15 AM

Although I had done a quick preview of the days calendar on entering the office, I double check the schedule, calculate the bills for outgoing guests and make sure we have prepared a unit for the new arrival scheduled for that afternoon. Two guests are leaving at 10:00 AM with one new arrival at 4:30 PM.

9:45 AM

First customer arrives early. People who have been on vacation just can't wait to get their hands on their little buddies and are frequently early. We have learned to just plan for this. Each kitty gets a final massage from me as I put them in their carrier. I swear they often look like they are giving their owner a smirky look that says they have had a perfectly good time on their vacation too. We find most cats return the affection they have received in like kind.

10:00 AM

Second customer arrives, picks up their kitty, and now Carol and I have the balance of the day to use as needed.

11:30 AM

We arrive at PetSmart to get dry and wet food, litter, and look at the kitties in the adoption area operated by Papa's Pet Project, a local animal rescue group. We catch lunch out together, make a stop at Home Depot, the grocery store and arrive home at 2:30 PM.

3:30 PM

Julia, our eight year old is due on the bus at any moment. It will be about another hour after that before Mel gets home from kindergarten.

4:30 PM

Mel arrives on her bus, followed shortly by our customer and new guest. A short discussion with our customer about their vacation consumes about 15 minutes. Most of our customers have boarded their cats with us many times and they feel more like family than customers. We are very fond of them all and often know quite a bit about them and their families.

5:30 PM

Carol and Joe work on supper and discuss the day's activities with the girls who are hovering about concerned with what is on their supper menu.

6:30 PM

Girls doing homework, watching TV and getting attention from us one way or another.

7:30 PM

Girls off to bed for the night. Sweet quiet and peace.

8:30 PM

Joe checks on the kitties, feeds everybody their supper, resolves any issues (hairballs, you know, are a fact of life in the kitty house) and gets them ready for the night.

10:00 PM

Time for the keepers of the inn to check on the girls and make sure they are tucked in and then we hit the sack.

A normal day features many trips in and out of the boarding area and we use these visits to give cats some individual attention as needed. Cats that would like to have some "out" time from their units will be let out, one family at a time, for a little play time in the boarding area.

Our business, which typically averages about 10-12 cats per night only requires about an hour or so in the morning to clean up and feed the cats and take care of other minor details. Even when we have 20+ cats we are through cleaning and getting ready for visitors in less than 2 hours. We also spend 15 minutes to one half hour in the evening feeding everybody, administering medicines where called for, and making sure everybody is comfortable for the night

A kitty B&B is a perfect business to run out of your home. With all the enthusiasm pet owners have for their pets, it is a business that can carry you through a recession – because people may cut back on the money they spend on trips and take shorter trips closer to home – but they still want to have their furry little buddies lovingly cared for while they are away. Our experience is that they just budget this cost into what they are going to spend overall on their trip.

From a financial perspective, taking care of 15-20 cats a day at our present rate of $17.00 could generate between $255 – $340 per day, $1,785 – $2,380 per week, and $7,140 – $9,520 a month. Not bad for an average time investment of a couple of hours a day. Although we have never operated at full capacity all the time, we know others that have.

ARE YOU WELL SUITED TO RUNNING A FELINE B&B?

There are two very important characteristics for a B&B owner to possess:

1. You should like working with people.

2. You should like cats and enjoy working with them.

A kitty B&B is a people business first and foremost. A friendly outgoing manner and a caring attitude is critical to your future success. The furry little people you will be taking care of are beloved members of the family that owns them. Cat owners suffer much angst over leaving their cat at the boarding house. They are placing great trust in you by doing so, and they want to be sure you really care about them and their pet.

If you do not genuinely like working with people, and have difficulty empathizing with them over their worries about leaving their kitty, you probably better find another occupation. It will not take prospects long to figure out that your B&B is not the place for them.

Many people will want to come to visit your facility before committing to boarding their kitty, and you need to be sympathetic to their concerns and spend the necessary time with them to make sure they become comfortable with you and your facility. When it comes to safeguarding their precious friends, pet owners can sniff out a person who is faking it real fast. You need to spend the time to assure people, answer questions, talk about yourself, your interests and why you are running a kitty B&B to convince them they can trust you with their pet. People will talk with you at great length, and sometimes much of the discussion may seemingly have little to do with cats, but in a way it does, because the pet owner is trying very hard to "scope" you out. They are desperately searching to see if they can convince themselves that they can place their trust in you. For example, we can sense many of our visitors feel very differently about us when we talk about the children we have provided specialized foster care for over twenty years. As we tell stories about the children, people can tell we really cared about them, and you can almost see them relaxing as they develop a better feel for the kind of people we are. If we can care about other people's children, they believe we're probably being honest about our feelings for cats too.

It should go without saying you also need to be genuinely interested in the animals. Most of the cats we care for are really nice kitties, but we do have some that will put us "through hoops" so to speak. Some cats can become aggressive under certain conditions, and many people know their cat will get "his undies in a bunch" when put into a boarding environment. If you tell them their kitty was a sweet little darling from the git go they will have a pretty good idea you are not telling the real story. When I have a kitty that puts me through the ropes, I tell people a couple of stories about how kitty put me in my place and they almost always get a big kick out of it. They know it's the truth. Of course, usually by the time people get back to pick up their kitty, the cat and I have come to some kind of understanding, especially where I am their source of food every day. Customers appreciate our efforts to build a good relationship with their little friend.

The above two characteristics are the most important factors in developing customers for your business. A close third is keeping your B&B scrupulously clean. One of our lady customer's dad is a vet. On a recent visit she observed, "It is always so clean here. It never smells like a kennel at all." Well, we work hard to keep it clean, because that tells people a lot about what kind of business we run. We also don't want odors in our house, since the boarding area is in the building. Paying close attention to cleanliness and demonstrating a caring attitude has helped us build a very good reputation in our area with both customers and local veterinarians.

Another characteristic required is to not mind getting your hands dirty. Cleaning up after cats, scooping litter boxes, cleaning down units and used potty boxes is all part of the game.

Having empathy for kitties if they develop a health problem while visiting is critical. I always feel terrible if a kitty has a health issue while it is with us. I dreaded this situation because I felt people would be mad at us. That has never happened. We do whatever is necessary to take good care of the kitty, including taking it to the vet if we are in doubt. People come back and profusely thank us for our dedication to caring for their cat and doing whatever had to be done in their absence to help the cat get better. People appreciate we went the extra mile when they weren't available to look after their cat's health, and they are thankful we cared enough to make sure their pet got the care they would have given it if they had been here.

There are other desirable characteristics, but the above are the highest priority. Others, mostly related to the management of the business will be covered when we get to that area of the book.

CHAPTER 3

CATNAP

"The Journey Home"

It was a bitter cold January morning when I first heard Mrs. Black and White's mournful cry. Ice covered the cranberry bog and the previous night's dusting of snow had turned the fields and woods into a winter wonderland. The thermometer had plummeted, finally stabilizing around 10°F. It was a hard time for a kitty without a warm hearth to cozy up to.

Even in the heart of winter, we crack open the windows in our boarding area to let in fresh air – an important ingredient in preventing the spread of feline respiratory ailments. The escaping odor of food and contented meowing sounds made by our guests are conveyed to the world beyond.

On this particular morning, a very nervous stray, evidently driven by sheer desperation, was sitting at the far end of the front porch. Meowing pitifully, she moved her head back and forth, sniffing air currents telegraphing the presence of food – food so maddeningly close, and yet, at the same time, because of her paralyzing fear of humans, so far away.

We had seen this kitty around the yard during the fall, usually on the hill overlooking the pool, or out back near the barn. She looked like she could be a stray, but was evidently finding sufficient nourishment during the good weather to get by. We had named her Mrs. Black and White, a name suggested by the contrast between her mostly black coat and one tiny, almost invisible patch of white on her head. As winter approached and the weather steadily became more severe, we noted her condition was markedly deteriorating with each subsequent sighting.

On this first morning, and for many mornings thereafter, we placed a dish with a serving of both dry and wet food at the far end of the porch in the hopes of helping her through her trial. The food was always gone by late morning, and within a couple of weeks we began to see her from time to time near the dish. Whenever possible, we would talk to her from the window as she ate hoping to establish some measure of rapport. Poor Mrs. Black and White would sit there, in pouring rain and driving snow, and devour every speck of food in that dish. Early on though, she made it quite clear she was not going to permit us to get any closer than absolutely necessary in order to get that meal.

She was such a pitiful sight we quickly became laden with guilt, feeling much like an unfit parent that had come to realize how neglectful their behavior had been. Our remorse spurred us to move the dish of food under the covered portion of the large front porch even though it would be much closer to the windows and the entrance door. She would have to approach a little closer to humans than she wanted, but we hoped that hunger would over-come fear and she could eat protected from the elements. Hunger, as it turned out, would carry the day.

As the weeks slipped by, I progressively moved the dish closer to the large glassed entry door to our B & B. By slowly acclimating her to our presence, we hoped we could eventually capture her and locate a family to provide a solution for her homeless plight. Mrs. Black and White's food dish progressed steadily to the point it was only five feet from and directly in front of the door. At that point, as long as I stood motionless inside, she would permit me to watch as she jumped over the porch rail and cautiously approached the food dish, her eyes riveted on me to detect the slightest movement. She looked like a coiled spring ready to explode at the slightest provocation.

Since our morning schedule with our kitty guests is quite predictable, Mrs. Black and White had soon adjusted her own daily priorities so as to be ready for breakfast to be served on the "terrace dining room," as we began to call it, by 9:00 a.m. And Mrs. Black and White had made it quite clear her preference was for a down-home lumberjack style breakfast.

One morning, having encountered a number of delays, I was far behind on my routine of serving up the morning meal. As I worked, I kept hearing this strange squeaking, scratching sound. Since it was very faint, and did not appear to be coming from any of our guest condos, I was not prompted to investigate immediately. The sound continued unabated as I worked.

Leaving our "kitchen" area heading for the condos I paused to open the interior office door to let the morning sunshine pour in and was startled by the sight greeting me. There, standing at her full height and patiently scratching up and down, over and over again on the glass storm door, was Mrs. Black and White. It seemed she was becoming more comfortable with our relationship after all.

At this point Mrs. Black and White became a real challenge. We had crossed an invisible "line-in-the-sand" she had put down in our relationship, and now winning her total trust and friendship and finding her a safe, loving home became a top priority.

Each morning I would wait until I saw her outside. Getting down on my hands and knees, I would slowly slip open the door and slide the dish towards her. At first, as soon as the door moved, she would retreat across the porch, sit down, and then wait until my hand had been withdrawn and the door was fully closed. Only then would she cautiously walk up and start to devour the meal in her ravenous, signature manner. As she ate, I remained on my hands and knees behind the glass barrier that had become our mutual guarantee of appropriate behavior and talk to her in soothing tones, constantly repeating all those foolish inanities that we use to communicate with our feline friends.

There were times during this budding relationship that I began to wonder who was training who. One technique she developed at this point was to finish the heaping dish of food, then back off and sit down and stare at the dish, as if convinced it might magically refill itself. She would then slowly elevate her eyes until they met mine and once again lower her head and focus on the dish. But this little subterfuge also created another opportunity for me. I eased the storm door open and reached for the dish. As was her custom, she quickly backed off and sat down to watch me. After refilling the dish with food, I slipped the door open and slid the dish towards her. A few seconds after I withdrew my hand she quickly walked in and finished off her second platter of the morning. Each time we repeated this little dance, she seemed less and less worried about my presence.

Soon we had progressed to the point I could push the dish out the door and leave the door ajar with my hand just a few inches from the dish as I continued to whisper "sweet nothings" to her. Once again, she reached down deep into her inner reserves and summoned the courage to approach and eat, but with her eyes always riveted to that hand in the event it made any untoward advance.

One morning, just to see what would happen, I let my hand remain on the dish. She sat and watched me for what seemed an eternity. Then, ever so slowly, one cautious step at a time, she approached and began to eat.

The sense of satisfaction experienced in gaining the trust of a fearful wild creature is exhilarating. Many animal lovers find it intoxicating. In spite of the joy of the accomplishment, however, the thought did spring to mind that one errant move on my part followed by a panic bite and I could be in considerable trouble. Cat bites are bad enough from an infection point of view, but rabies is also an ever-present threat with unvaccinated animals. But empathy for poor Mrs. Black and White's homeless predicament spurred me on.

Our "Dances with Felines" relationship climaxed the morning I was able to delicately lift my hand from the dish while she was eating and ever so lightly brush my finger along the hair on top of her head. The result of this little maneuver was electrifying – for both of us. As soon as she realized what was happening she exploded backwards in one convulsive leap, landing two or three feet away from the dish. I banged by head on the door jamb as my own reflex action propelled me back inside the door. Then she just sat down and glared at me. I was sure I knew exactly what she was thinking.

"No more sweet talk, buster! We had an agreement, remember – no touching!"

The look in her eyes seemed to be one of slight confusion; an odd mixture of fear, appreciation and a bit of trust due to the fact I had never done anything but help her through her ordeal. But the fear that was so deeply ingrained within her that she might never be able to trust a human again was a battle yet remaining to be won.

It did seem though that the time had finally arrived to make our move to capture our little friend and find her a happy, loving home.

At this point, Mrs. Black and White vaporized.

Search as we might, we could not catch a glimpse of her anywhere. Week after week rolled by. I would open the door each morning hoping to set my eyes on that little black kitty and know she was ok, but to no avail.

We began to blame ourselves. Had we waited too long? Did she get hit by a car? Had one of the coyotes that are becoming an increasing problem in our area ended her journey? We also feared that she could have become ill and had no none to care for her. Or, had she sensed what we were up to, in a way humans can't quite grasp, and decided to move on?

Week after week we watched. Gradually we began to accept the fact we might never know the fate of Mrs. Black and White.

As the harshness of winter began to fade and the warmth of the spring sun was improving our outlook on life, Mrs. Black and White was slowly starting to become a distant memory.

I had begun to work in earnest on our book at that point, and was spending significant amounts of time at my computer. We were fast approaching Memorial Day, a time when the warmth of the sun frequently clashes with cool ocean temperatures here on the coast and produces fog. The fog that morning was heavy, imparting an ethereal quality to the landscape, a scene where plants and trees seemed to have found a source of locomotion as they drifted in and out of the ghostly mist. Carol's voice startled me when she called,

"Come quickly, I want to show you something."

"Look", she said, "up there, on top of the wall."

Walking along the top of the wall, fading in and out of the mist was a jet-black kitty. As she moved towards us out of the mist, we strained to see if it could possibly be Mrs. Black and White. Then she turned her face toward us, and the tell-tale little spot of white on her head became visible. It was Mrs. Black and White, and she looked in amazingly good condition. Her frame had filled out and the bony rib cage she once carried as a badge of courage was no longer there. Her coat had a luxurious shine to it, and she appeared bright eyed, alert, and not too concerned about our watching. Around her neck was a bright red collar complete with dangling rabies tag and a little bell.

Evidently, it would seem, someone else had the same idea for Mrs. Black and White's future we did, but they must have executed their plan just a bit before we were ready to launch our own.

It's always a joy to find the ending to one of these stories about God's little creatures is a happy one. All the work we had poured into Mrs. Black and White had not, after all, been in vain. Although not by our hand, our dreams for Mrs. Black and White had come true.

Although we would never see her again, I often wonder if she made that one last visit to let us know that she appreciated what we had done for her. It was almost as if she was saying "Thank you and goodbye."

The warm hearth and loving family we had hoped to find for her had become a reality.

Good luck, Mrs. Black and White, and thanks for letting us know that our efforts had not been in vain.

CHAPTER 4

BUSINESS PLANNING FOR
A KITTY B&B

ANALYZING YOUR MARKET AREA'S POTENTIAL.

Location, location, location is a real estate axiom. The location of a cat B&B is a vital factor in its eventual success. You need to have a sufficient population and suitable demographics in your target market area to succeed. Whether you are starting your business at your current home's location or evaluating another site, a detailed Market Analysis is a crucial step in making a final decision on opening a business.

Evaluating the health of an industry sector (pet care) and sub-sectors (boarding/kenneling) is important. Understanding how the industry's health relates to the specific geographic market area in which you will be opening your business is critical. The process involved of determining the potential of any specific geographic area is referred to as Target Market Analysis.

Now the question becomes, "How can you estimate the business potential for the area." The following section demonstrates the methodology used by most sophisticated marketers to analyze area demographics and business potential before they finalize a geographic location. This process helps to evaluate the potential of a location being considered for establishing a business. The data required to perform such an analysis can be easily accessed on the Internet.

In many cases, since the cat B&B is a relatively small business, the owner will likely be considering running the business on property already owned, such as a modified garage, lower level in the home or even a wing of the home as we have done at Pampered Cats. Whether you are selecting a location or attempting to determine the potential of an existing location, the evaluation process is the same.

We will run through the process using our own business as an example for a couple of reasons. One reason is we are familiar with our area and its idiosyncrasies, making it a bit faster to prepare the tutorial. A second reason is our site provides a unique example of one of the potential pitfalls to be aware of.

FIGURE 1 – MAP SHOWING SELECTION OF MARKET AREA

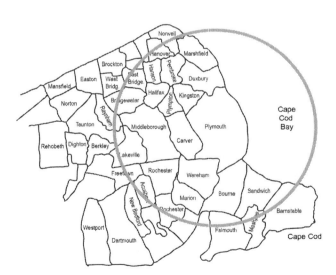

In general, the bulk of the customers for a cat hotel will reside within a 20-mile radius of the business location. The accompanying Figure 1 (preceding page) shows the location of our property. One of its major benefits is that it is located only 1500 feet from the shore of Cape Cod Bay. One of the biggest challenges our business faces is it is located only 1500 feet from the shore of Cape Cod Bay. Our 20-mile radius to the northeast, east, and southeast is populated only by seagulls, fish and seals - and lately by a few great white sharks, none of which are very good potential customers. Our particular physical property was so well suited to the B&B concept however, we decided to proceed and live with the limits our location would place on future business development. If we had human population to the north, northeast, and southeast however, we would probably be doing at least 25%-35% more volume. Our market analysis did show that there was a sufficient population within the 20-mile radius to support the business at a level we were comfortable with.

The information needed for analysis purposes can be gleaned from the U. S. Census data and the National Pet Owners Survey complied by The American Pet Products Association (APPA).

The 2011-2012 National Pet Owners Survey compiled by APPA showed:

1. There are approximately 78.2 million pet dogs in the US

2. There are approximately 86.4 million pet cats in the US

3. 33% of US Households (HH) own 1 cat

4. 52% of cat owners have more than one cat

5. 2.2 cats is the average number of cats owned by cat owning households.

Next, determine the population and number of households located within a 20-mile radius of your location. The following table shows a number of towns within a 20-mile location of our business, Pampered Cats. We have limited the number selected to simplify the process of performing the analysis.

Keep in mind the population and household numbers are never absolute. Census data is often being adjusted long after the census is completed, and you will find incomplete data in some areas. The objective is to get the best representation possible for the towns surrounding the target location. Use numbers from earlier census results if necessary. Towns do not usually change by orders of magnitude in short periods of time. You will find Wikipedia has information on their site regarding census data. If you are aware of some dramatic changes going on in the subject area look for the latest possible figures from some local sources.

FIGURE 2 - TOWNS WITH POPULATIONS, HOUSEHOLDS, HOUSEHOLDS OWNING CATS AND TOTAL CAT POPULATION.

TOWN	*POP.	*HH's	HHs W/CATS	CAT. POP.
Plymouth	56.5	18.4	6,100	13,358
Kingston	12.6	4.3	1,419	3,121
Duxbury	15	4.9	1,617	3,557
Marshfield	25.1	8.9	2,937	6,461
Carver	11.5	3.9	1,287	2,831
Wareham	21.8	8.2	2,706	5,953
Bourne	19.7	7.4	2,442	5,372
Lakeville	10.6	3.3	1,089	2,395
	172.80	59.30	19,597	43,048

* Population and Households in thousands

Just type the name of the town and the state postal abbreviation (MA for example) in the Wikipedia search box and you will be surprised what you can find out about demographics. The same information entered in the Google search box will usually result in listings including the town name, related articles and a Wikipedia link. Once on the WikiPedia page, look for the demographic link. If that does not work, type "demographics" (without the quotes) then the town and state abbreviation as shown here: (demographics Plymouth ma) in the Wikipedia search box and one of the first few links suggested should take you to the demographic information for the town.

The statistics in Figure 2 were constructed in the manner described below. The Town of Plymouth, MA, has 18.4K Households. APPA says that on a nationwide basis .33 of households own cats. So we multiply .33 X 18.4 and come up with approximately 6,072 HHs that own cats. Since the national survey determined, on average, that 2.2 cats are owned by each cat owning household, we multiply 2.2 X 6,072 and come up with a projected cat population of 13,358 in Plymouth. Follow the same process for each community within your 20-mile radius.

APPA's 2011-2012 study surveyed cat owners and found approximately $166.00 was spent by each respondent for kenneling services. That would result in an expenditure of over one million dollars in Plymouth, a total I find doubtful, but these statistics are only guides. Also keep in mind respondents may have included pet sitting services in their answer to the kenneling question. Many people board cats with their vet, or kennels that host both dogs and cats, so there is competition for those dollars.

At the date of writing, there are three cat-only boarding facilities competing for the business in these towns. Some of the other facilities draw from a wider area due to their location, so these numbers do not represent the total pie for all three facilities. The overall market for all three facilities covers a much larger area than just the towns we have listed for our own location.

As mentioned earlier we have lost approximately 30% of what could be our market territory due to our location directly on the ocean, but we still have a profitable business. We also have two of our state's largest luxury home communities located in the town, and the affluent residents of these communities are prime prospects for our services.

There are many other factors to evaluate. If the surrounding towns have very low-income demographics, it will affect the business negatively. If the population is sparse that will impact the business. High-income demographics will increase potential substantially, because the more affluent residents can afford to board their cats without being concerned about cost. Their most important concern will be knowing their cat is well cared for and comfortable in the environment at your boarding facility.

THE MARKET AREA COMPETITIVE SURVEY

Once the location's market area has been analyzed and sufficient potential has been found to proceed, the next step will be to conduct a Market Area Competitive Survey. At a minimum, every cat-only B&B within a thirty mile radius of the intended location should be visited. Also include at least a few kennels that board both dogs and cats to get a good feeling for the accommodations those facilities offer. If there are any truly luxurious boarding facilities within 60 miles of the site under consideration, visit them. A lot can be learned about how such businesses operate and ideas can be obtained for one's own business.

Typically, once a good reputation is established, the business will draw the bulk of its customers from within a 20-mile radius. As your reputation grows, people will be willing to travel 30 miles or more to board their kitty. We have customers that travel 50 miles plus to board their kitties with us, and it is not unusual to find customers that will travel even further than that. As the years go by, we find people coming from increasingly greater distances.

Conducting the competitive survey is not rocket science. Just call, as if you are a potential customer that wants to board your cat, and say you would like to come and visit before making boarding arrangements. It is very common for potential customers to call boarding facilities to take a tour. It is part of the daily routine in the boarding business. Don't be self conscious about this endeavor. People in the cat care business are usually very cordial people and like to talk about what they do. This is a critically important step and should not be sidestepped.

Obtain each facility's brochure or flyer. Make sure to get a price list of boarding costs. Most will have a price for two, three, or four or more cats that can board in the same condo in addition to the single cat charge. Find out what the cost is if you have two cats that cannot be boarded together because they fight. Make mental notes about each operation, such as overall condo size, number of shelves and how shelves are arranged along with approximate sizes, door types (Plexiglas, screened) and materials used to build the units. Note the amount of fabrics used in the boarding area. Fabrics are more difficult to disinfect than hard, smooth surfaces, and extensive use of fabrics in a facility will create a lot of work. Prospects might like the look of fabric, but from a cat health point of view, solid surfaces that can be easily and thoroughly disinfected is the far better route. We believe the less fabric we have to deal with the better. You can utilize small lightweight blankets and easy to launder beds to provide the cozy warmth such items convey.

Encourage people to bring their kitty's favorite bed or blanket from home. Kitty will be more comfortable and you will save a lot of money and work on laundry activities.

Ventilation capability is important to keeping kitty guests healthy. Find out what kind of provisions each facility has made for ventilating their boarding areas.

All this information is helpful in planning the design of units. We incorporated many of the features uncovered in our research into our B&B design to strengthen our competitive position.

Other items of interest include any additional services offered, such as playtime, med applications (including insulin shots), grooming, etc. What does each service cost? Make sure to make notes on the flyer or write information down as soon as you get to your car, because by the end of the day features and facilities will start blending together in your memory and it will be hard to keep it all straight.

It is not a bad idea to tour a couple of really extravagant boarding operations even if you do not intend to build that kind of facility. Seeing what they offer and how they operate will be helpful to your overall view of the business.

When you have completed your survey trips, prepare a chart that lists the features and other information for each facility.

Now you are prepared to evaluate just how your facility will fit into the boarding picture in your market area. Where will you be stronger than your competition? Where will you be weaker? Can you build in additional features as you design your facility to enhance your position?

Next, give some thought to where you will fit into the price matrix for the area. For our facility, we chose to set our rates above our two major competitors because we have strengths that are highly desirable to our target audience that the competition does not posses. Our major advantage is our cat boarding facility is a true B&B since our boarding area is located in a wing of our house. The cats have people in the building with them on an almost 24-7 basis. Customers really like this. We are in and out of the boarding area throughout the day and evening. My office, where I am writing now, is right next to the cat boarding room. Our two major competitors board the cats in separate buildings on their property – with one in particular located quite a distance from the residence. This factor has been mentioned to me a number of times when people come in to tour that have seen the other kennel. You can charge more when you have this kind of advantage. By the same token, we are less expensive than many of the other commercial facilities in the area since they are high overhead operations, with expensive commercial space and many employees. Our customers know that my wife and I are the only two people that work with the cats, that we love the cats and deal with each cat based on their unique personality.

COMPETITIVE PRICE CHART.

A Competitive Market Survey provides the rates other are charging for their services in the area. Carefully analyze the prices charged by each facility by comparing those prices to the services they offer and the attractiveness of the facility. Lower pricing when combined with tiny wire cages won't appeal to people looking for a "quality boarding experience." A facility with tiny wire cages and outdoor views defeats the purpose of the outdoor views, because cats are particularly threatened when they are exposed on all four sides and overhead in the presence of other cats. This is a high-stress environment for the cats. As you analyze the competition, you will begin to get a feel for where your facility fits into the overall scheme of things, and then you just have to set what you consider is a fair price for what you have to offer. But remember, the host's enthusiasm, caring attitude and willingness to go the extra mile is part of the equation, and don't forget to consider that factor in setting your rates. Things like willingness to help people with a tough travel schedule, or someone who has a break down on the road but still has to be somewhere the next morning and needs to get their cat at an inconvenient hour goes a long way to building a great customer relationship. We have had cats picked up at 10:00 pm because someone had an unexpected emergency. We don't encourage late pickups because we need a life too, but there are times when going the extra mile helps build a life-long relationship.

ACTUALLY SETTING YOUR RATES.

In the end the marketplace will dictate what you can actually get for your services. You can set your rates as high as you want, but if the market won't pay for it you are not going to succeed. You give yourself the best chance for success by setting a reasonable price related to both the market area you serve and where you fit into the spectrum of features and benefits offered by the available facilities.

BUSINESS PLANNING AND BUSINESS PLANS.

Lots of people are big into business plans. If you've never run a business before writing a plan is probably a good idea. The process will help you put flesh on the bones of your operation and assist in identifying questions and potential weaknesses you can deal with early on.

My background includes business and marketing management as well as prior experience running my own business. After managing million dollar marketing and advertising campaigns for both large consumer and industrial products companies, I was comfortable with operating my small home based business without a formal written plan. We did create a five-year operating financial forecast along with detailed business startup cost projections.

If you find the prospect of starting and operating a simple home-based business a daunting task, writing a good plan will be worth the time and effort you put into it.

A number of business plan templates/software are available on the internet, but there is no need to pay a lot of money for sophisticated business planning software packages. Microsoft has prepared a number of templates for use with Microsoft Word for preparing business plans. Microsoft also offers Excel templates for financial budgets and forecasts. These are available on the Microsoft web site at the following URL:

http://www.wordtemplates.org/business-word-templates/sample-business-plan-templates/

Copy and paste the above URL into your web browser URL bar. Once on the Microsoft page you can click the download button to get the specific template needed. Other templates are also offered.

A few more templates for business/marketing plans can be loct-ed by simply searching for "free business plan templates. There are numerous sites offering a wide range of planning templates. Start with the above Microsoft URL and then search through their site to view all the business planning tools that are available at no cost.

START-UP COSTS AND BUDGET

Once physical specifications are roughed out for a facility bud-get costs can be established.

A cat boarding facility does not require extensive equipment. The major consideration is having appropriate enclosures in which to accommodate the cats. Cat boarding facilities have evolved steadily over the years since we started our business and some fa-cilities have gone very upscale, featuring units surrounded by in-terior gardens, lavish furniture and more. We find, at least in our area, people's major concerns are for their kitty to have comfort-able accommodations and that the pet owner feels totally com-fortable with the caretakers. I believe there are two major reasons our business has prospered. The first is that the facility itself is unusual, attractive and appealing to both cat owners and cats. The second is that people sense we love and care for their cats with the same level of enthusiasm we have for our own. People want their kitties to have the best possible "vacation" and most pet owners are willing to pay a premium for the best facility.

If you are handy doing carpentry work, building the cat condos is a fairly easy task to accomplish. If there is sufficient interest we plan on preparing a Cat Boarding Operation Manual that will pro-vide detailed plans to help facilitate building units. The manual will include material lists, suppliers of the special fasteners required, specs for door screens, tools required or helpful, and more to assist with building condos. If you are going to have units custom built, the specifications provided in our manual will help to simplify ob-taining bids from suppliers.

One additional area of concern is ventilation. Adequate air ventilation is critical in a boarding facility to keep animals healthy. If I were building a facility today, I would install a ventilation system with air exchanger and HEPPA air filters for air quality control. More details on this subject will be available in the Pampered Cats Cat Boarding Operation Manual.

TOWN APPROVALS.

Checking with the town (or applicable zoning authority office) before proceeding with the B&B plan is important. Regulations vary by city or town, county and state, and it is important to make sure operating a kitty B&B on the selected property will be approved.

Obtaining a license to operate or a business certificate may also be required. Licensing may be the responsibility of either state or local government authorities in charge of animal care facilities. Check with local authorities to obtain all the information needed.

Today, a business certificate or license is required by banks to open a business checking account, a regulation imposed due to money laundering and terrorist threats since 9/11.

Town approvals may also be required for any signage to be erected. We found the strategy of using temporary real estate type signs (both the metal frame "stick-in-the-ground" type as well as the traditional 4"x4" post with hanging sign) have worked for us with no problem and no approvals. We started with the stick-in metal frame and then after a year or so installed the 4"x4" post with hanging sign version.

BUSINESS INSURANCE

It is a good idea to have a business insurance package to cover a B&B. A suitable policy can provide protection for possible physical injury to a customer and for damage to the building, fixtures, etc. Available options can cover a wide range of possibilities, including noncollectable account receivables, business interruption (income replacement) and more. Consult an insurance agent for more information. Contact us for specific information if needed. The Pampered Cats Cat Boarding Manual will provide information on at least one company that writes these policies as this type of coverage is getting difficult to locate.

In the following paragraphs we look at additional related service areas and ideas to explore to increase revenues.

PET GROOMING

If the innkeeper has the experience or desire to learn grooming skills, grooming guests staying at the inn could add substantial income to the business. Those who don't want to groom could work out an agreement with a mobile groomer that can come to the inn to do the work in the mobile groomers van or in your facility if you have the space available.

Performing the service oneself would provide the most income, but for those uncomfortable in that role, especially since some cats can be "wildly resistant" at times to those trying to care for them, the professional grooming approach may be best. Negotiate a professional discount that allows for the inn to mark up the service to make a reasonable profit for the time and effort the process requires. If there is room for a separate grooming area, dogs could also be groomed as long as they are separated from the cats.

PET TAXI

A transportation service for pets is another potentially profitable service. Often times pet owners need pets transported to medical appointments, doggy day care, boarding, grooming and training appointments. Even though the inn may be operating as a "cats only" facility, that would not prevent providing a transportation service for a variety of pets.

YARD CLEANING.

Operating a "cat only" boarding facility could dovetail quite nicely with running a service such as Pooper Scooper Yard Cleaning. Many of your cat customers will have one or more dogs, and your contacts can open up opportunities to provide such services. Pooper Scooper has advertised their franchise yard cleaning service in our area's pet magazine for years.

SELLING SUPPLIES.

If room is available, selling supplies such as specialty foods, health foods and other cat oriented items that are not readily available at regular pet stores is a possibility. Visit sites such as http://www.cattoys.com/ It will provide ideas for special items to sell. Catnip "cigars," gourmet catnip, squeaky mouses and more all may be purchased by customers for their cats to enjoy while they stay at the inn. Small beds that fit well into condos might be purchased by people that overlooked bringing a bed for their baby's vacation. Check zoning license restrictions as retail sales may not be allowed in some areas, especially where some sort of zoning variance has been granted. Many zoning boards will allow a B&B in certain residential areas, but will not allow retail sales. Product sales also require collecting and paying Sales Taxes, something not required for boarding services in many areas to date.

PET PHOTOGRAPHY

Many boarding facilities for dogs, cats and other pets offer pet portrait services as a way to expand income. For innkeepers interested in photography and who have the patience for it, pet portraits can bring in some pretty good money. Contracting with someone who specializes in pet photography to come in and take the photos is also a possibility. A wholesale price can be negotiated that the inn can markup to make a profit without having to do all the work.

PET ART PORTRAITS

Art portraits of pets done in watercolor, pastels, oil, pencil, and even computerized art are all popular. Many of the artists work from a provided photo. Artists working in all these art forms in in any area can be found with a simple web search. Hanging a few samples of their work in the boarding office should suffice to provoke interest.

Although there are other areas that could be explored, the previous paragraphs provide a good example of available opportunities to increase sales for owners who wish to venture further afield.

PET SITTING.

You probably think of pet sitting as being the competition to a boarding facility, and that's true – to a point. If an inn is a "cats only" boarding facility, it will be more difficult to expand into providing dog boarding and still maintain an exclusive image as being for cats only. By expanding into pet sitting, the business can care for all the other pets that need care when people travel, potentially dramatically increasing potential revenue. It pays to think out-of-the-box when it comes to looking at new opportunities.

CAT BOARDING OR CAT SITTING?

There are advantages and disadvantages to both cat boarding and cat sitting. Some cat owners don't mind having someone going in and out of their home while they are away, others do.

Our perspective, naturally, favors the boarding approach, and since most readers of this book are probably considering opening a boarding facility, our discussion will focus on the boarding perspective.

When some cats are left at home, they will do ok for a while. Others get freaked out when that very important person they depend on for all things disappears – especially if they are left alone for many days with just short visits by pet sitters. People-friendly cats will have a difficult time when they are left alone, and they have a tendency to get into trouble once they get upset. A few will get outright mad and do quite a bit of damage. The stories in the next couple of pages have been related to us by our customers and will give you an idea of the types of things that can happen when pet owners are away.

RYE AND THE GREAT FLOOD

Rye was a big Bengal cat that loved to play with water. A running faucet was nirvana as far as Rye was concerned. Rye's owner, Lori, had made a reservation, then called and canceled as she felt Rye probably would be fine at home. After all, they would only be gone two days (one overnight). Alone and bored, Rye became intrigued by the new faucet just installed in the upstairs bath. The faucet had one of those long, gracefully curved handles that ascended far above the sink. With plenty of time to work, Rye figured out how to push that long handle up and get the water running.

When Lori and her husband returned Monday morning, they were horrified to see water running from under the front door. In a panic, Bill raced around back, and found water seeping out from under the back door too. Once inside the house they could only stare in disbelief at the sagging ceilings and ruined floors. Water was pouring down the stairs, as if a new water feature had been installed upstairs during their absence. Bill could hear the water running as he ran up the stairs and found the new faucet running full tilt, water flowing out of the sink and down onto the floor. (The overflow in the new sink was defective).

Rye's little escapade caused in excess of $30,000 worth of damage in the short time he was "home alone."

THERE ARE MANY WAYS TO PUNISH YOUR OWNER.

Lori and Bill now have a new cat, Bella. Friends volunteered to come over and tend Bella for a couple of days recently while Bill and Lori were away for a long weekend. Bella sleeps with Bill and Lori, but the friends closed the bedroom door at night, arousing Bella's ire. A few days after their return Lori noticed a bad aroma in the house. She searched but could find nothing. Pausing by one of her little blanket lined decorator baskets, she noticed the odor seemed stronger. Leaning over to sniff the basket she was greeted by the acrid odor of week old cat urine. Bella, a fastidiously clean little kitty, miffed at being banished from the bedroom, exhibited her displeasure with the sleeping arrangements by making a donation in every basket she could find.

WILL AND THE GREAT AMERICAN INDIAN ARTIFACT COLLECTION

Then there was Will, a great big handsome black and white long furred cat. His dad left him home alone for a couple of days. After getting bored, he climbed the curtains, tearing them off the wall. Looking for a new challenge, he started chewing on dad's precious collection of Indian artifacts displayed on the fireplace mantle. Mind you, Will had ignored these objects for years, but he knew how to show his displeasure in a way that really hurt. Will spent a lot of time at the "cat house" after that weekend.

LEAVING YOUR CAT AT SOMEONE ELSE'S HOME.

Sam is what we would call a "scaredy cat." When Amy dropped Sam off at her parent's house he immediately went into hibernation, absolutely terrified of anybody coming near him. This is a somewhat common (but at times hazardous) feline reaction to a strange environment. Since Sam was not confined to any one room, he was difficult to set an eye on at best, but then he totally disappeared. A week went by and not a sign of him. Amy's parents searched and called, but no Sam.

Amy and her husband Bob returned and came over and searched and called, but no Sam. Sam's food and water had now been untouched for a week.

Realizing they had been working in the attic at one point when Sam was visiting, Amy's parents searched the attic, but to no avail. The attic stairs were left down in the hope that if Sam was up there, he would come down on his own when things were quiet. Over the second weekend Amy and Bob were back again hoping for a miracle. Even though she thought it to be a waste of time, Amy ascended the attic stairs one more time. As she crouched down, she thought she heard a slight rustling sound. She kneeled on the floor and talked in soothing tones. She heard another rustle. Staring intently down along the joists, deep under the eaves, two barely discernible eyes began to materialize. Ever so slowly a very bedraggled Sam crawled out of the darkness. Everybody concluded Sam must have caught a few mice in the attic of that old house for sustenance during his ordeal, because he looked in better shape than he should have considering how long he had been AWOL.

SUMMARY.

In addition to the foregoing types of problems there are other concerns. Safety is the first. A malfunctioning furnace generating carbon dioxide can quickly snuff out your pet's life when there is no one home to help. The blaring CO^2 monitor will not help kitty. My wife lost her pets when she was in high school because the pets were alone when a fire broke out in her parent's house.

We've had customers that had their cat get out of the house on the pet sitter or visiting caregiver and the cat was never seen again. Unfortunately, pet sitters and other visitors have things to do and they can't stay at your house for days waiting for kitty to decide if it is going to return home.

When boarding a cat, the kitty will have people around most of the time. The person caring for them notices changes in their behavior and can keep an eye on their food consumption, litter box and overall health just like the pet owner does at home. They get socialization and loving care, something most of the cats respond to. The few that are antisocial get a really nice "hidey-hole-bed" so they can stay secluded if they wish. Some will come out when they get comfortable and make a new friend or two, but the ball is in their court.

Then there are those situations where cats are on medications. At home they can give the sitter or friend the slip real easy if they don't want to take their meds. As soon as they hear someone coming, they vanish. When boarding, they take their meds as ordered by the doc.

There are times when pet sitting may offer an advantage. For example, you will find situations where people just cannot get their cats into a carrier. One lady customer of ours got so scratched up by her cat Pokey she just didn't want to even try to get him in a carrier. When she called us, she was in a quandary. Pokey was not going into any carrier and the time was fast approaching for her flight to leave. She called and told us the problem and asked if we had any advice. Then she asked, "Would you come to the house and feed Pokey while I am gone. I will pay you the boarding fee you were going to charge." We could empathize with her plight. One basic premise of a service business is that your only reason for existence is to SERVE your customers. "Just drop your key off on the way to the airport and we will take care of Pokey for you." You could feel the relief in her voice over the phone.

Well, we have regularly pet sat for Pokey a number of times and the agreement has made Pokey and his owner happy and worked well for us too. I am sure if we wanted to promote pet sitting and go after the business we could do well at it.

CHAPTER 5

DESIGNING AND BUILDING
THE CAT B&B

As with all endeavors, the hardest thing to do most of the time to just get started. Inertia is great when it is working for you, but a challenge when working against you. Once you get going there are a number of things that can be done concurrently with building the inn.

Before starting on construction, the following two steps should always have been completed:

1. Obtained a Zoning Permit to ensure municipality will permit operation of the business in selected location.

2. Obtained Business and or licensing permits required for animal boarding by the state, county, or municipality to meet legal requirements for operating this type of business.

There is no sense in starting construction only to find you will not be allowed to operate in the intended location.

PREPARATION FOR DESIGNING THE B&B.

As previously discussed, we cannot overemphasize the importance of visiting every cat boarding facility in your area. It is important to see what each physical facility looks like and how it operates. Visit these businesses as if you have a need to board your cat.

Visiting as a potential customer provides a number of benefits. This approach will give you a much better feeling for how the whole process operates if you have never boarded a pet. You will be asked the questions facilities need to have answered to board a kitty. These are the questions you will need to ask prospective customers in the near future. Carefully observe the physical facility and the condos in which your kitty would be residing. Would you be happy with your cat staying in them? If the answer is yes, what do you like? If the answer is no, what do you dislike? You will want to factor all this information into your decision making process as you plan and build your facility.

As you visit a boarding business, what is your reaction to the people you are dealing with? What do you like about how they treat you? What do you dislike? Do they mention the names of the animals as they show you around? Do they seem to resent spending time with you, or act as if they are in a hurry and need to get on to something else? Do they patiently answer your questions? All this information will assist you in preparing to work with visitors to your own facility.

With all of the above information in hand, you can set out to create an environment in your kitty B&B that will favorably compare to your competition.

GETTING INTO THE DESIGN PROCESS.

Once we had a general idea of how we wanted our B&B to look and feel, we began the process of actually laying out the boarding rooms. We were very impressed with the facility we had seen featured in Yankee Magazine. It seemed to be just the kind of kitty B&B we wanted to create. Since the owner's property and business were for sale, we called to ask some questions. During the conversation she offered to let us "shadow" her for a day so we could see how she handled things. She also offered to sell us a manual she had created on how to start a kitty B & B facility. The total cost for the day along with the manual was $400.00 (that was 18 years ago). It was a good investment, as it saved us time and energy and helped us avoid many potential pitfalls in the design and start-up process. Although it did not provide any where near the amount of information we plan on incorporating in our Pampered Cats Cat Boarding Manual (which we hope to publish in the near future) it was a good investment at the time and served its purpose well.

We had decided on the rooms in the wing of our home that would be used for boarding, so we began the process of laying out the condos. We took the unit measurements from the manual we had purchased and laid them out on the floor along the longest side of the room, outlining each unit with masking tape. Then we did the same thing along the adjacent wall and adjusted the spaces until we were satisfied. The condos were then constructed as built-ins fitting into the outlined floor plan. When we subsequently added more condos we utilized a modular approach. The modular units were much easier and faster to complete than our original built-in units. Our Pampered Cats Cat Boarding Manual will include plans for both approaches, but we would recommend you seriously consider the modular design. The manual will include instructions on how to build the units, materials to use, and special hardware that will make the job much easier to accomplish.

At the time we were laying out the units we were also making our ambiance/décor decisions. We wanted to make to make our kitty B&B as friendly and homey as possible. We decided to use Minwax puritan pine stain for our doors and trim to achieve a warm cozy feeling. We then used contrasting white melamine for the interior of the units. The melamine has worked well, as it is bright and cheerful and projects a pristine, clean aura. The ease of cleaning allows us to scrupulously sanitize units between guests. We used wire mesh on the doors of the condos because we did not want the cats to feel "imprisoned" behind a wall of Plexiglas, a common design feature in many kennels. Light colored vinyl flooring with flecks of earth colors was chosen to keep the room bright but also help minimize visibility of the dust and dirt cats manage to track around the floor in spite of repeated vacuuming.

There is much more to consider, and the following section provides a look at many of these subjects.

THINGS TO CONSIDER WHEN DESIGNING YOUR B & B.

The following list is an overview of things to think about as you start putting your business together.

1. Lighting/Views - It is important to design the boarding area so it has plenty of natural light and windows with outside views. Interior lighting should be bright and cheerful. We have found that bright white fluorescent lighting can be a bit harsh in the boarding room. We prefer soft or warm white fluorescents as they enhance the cozy, homey feeling we want to project.

2. Ventilation/Heat/Air Conditioning - Providing plenty of fresh air is a must for a cat boarding facility. The best solution is an air exchange system that exhausts interior room air and imports fresh outside air. The system contains a heat exchange device that conserves both heat and cold from the outgoing air by transferring it to the incoming air, resulting in a minimum loss of energy. These units can be designed into an overall heating/cooling system, or an independent air exchange unit can be installed if required.

3. Kitchen Facility - A mini-kitchen area with sink and storage for cleaning supplies located in or near the boarding area is highly desirable. The facility we modeled ours on had their mini-kitchen installed in a large closet so the door could be closed and hidden from the view of visitors.

4. Feeding Station - You will find that a dedicated feeding station is a real necessity. An under counter kitchen cabinet unit with drawers for dishes and food storage works well for us. We installed a section of Formica® laminate counter top that resembles granite for a work surface.

5. Vacuum cleaner - A vacuum cleaner was a necessity for us to avoid being down on our knees with a dustpan and brush. A built in system installed in a concealed cabinet, closet, or adjacent room is ideal. An industrial canister type can be used if necessary. We have an Oreck® Industrial Canister that has served us without fail for 18 years now. Try to find a semi-secluded spot for the cannister if it is in the boarding room. We installed ours under one of our special units that has a two foot by two foot opening under the floor of the unit. The "crushproof" hose (believe me, it will get stepped on) is vital, and the hose needs to be long enough to reach all of the units in the boarding area.

6. Boarding Room Flooring - A cheerful, bright vinyl flooring material with enough pattern to minimize the dust and dirt that is part of life in a cat boarding facility is important. No matter how much one cleans, there are always specks of dirt from visitor's shoes, cats' feet, etc. Vinyl takes the abuse and spills and cleans up easily.

7. Food and Water Dishes - Glass dishes have been best for us. Aluminum and plastic dishes can cause allergy problems for some cats. Acne on the cats lower jaw is a typical reaction for those that are allergic to plastic or aluminum. We have always used Corningware dishes – good looking and tough – although it is getting harder and harder to find them.

8. Litter Boxes - We planned our condos so the height of the bottom shelf is sufficient to clear the top of the litter box WITH THE COVER ON. Litter boxes vary all over the place for height and length, so the bottom shelf should be at a height that accommodates a few different litter box brands and designs. Manufacturers keep changing designs and measurements, so you don't want to be pinned down to a particular box that may not be available in a couple of years. I can no longer find the boxes we designed our units to accommodate originally, but thankfully we allowed a bit of extra space and have been able to find substitutes. Get plenty of covers if litter pans don't come with one. You won't believe how many cats manage to pee over the top of an uncovered 5" high litter pan. Covers stop that problem and also help minimize the mess many cats make when they get "playing in the bathroom."

9. Cleaners/Disinfectants - Many cleaners and disinfectants can have a negative impact on cats' health. Bleach vapor - even just the left over odor - if not completely wiped down and neutralized with water, can cause cats to sneeze and develop breathing issues. We clean units with Nolvasan, a commercial kennel disinfectant, diluted according to manufacturer directions. Nolvasan is used by many veterinarians. We are careful to keep the solution off bare hands (use latex gloves) and avoid breathing the mist if any is created. We always set the spray bottle to stream rather than spray to protect ourselves from breathing the chemical vapors.

10. Protective Gloves - Protective gloves to handle panicked or aggressive cats prevent scratches and bites and have been a lifesaver at times. We have boarded very few cats that have attempted to bite, but some cats panic when you try to put them in a carrier, and their flailing paws can scratch you up real good. Kevlar gloves with arm covers that go up to the elbows provide excellent protection. We always protect ourselves when there is any in doubt. Remember the old adage, an ounce of prevention is worth a pound of cure.

11. Condo Shelf Padding - Carpet samples (approximately the 12"x18" size or whatever fits shelves) used on displays in carpet stores are excellent pads for the kitties to rest on. Many stores are glad to give them away to get rid of them or sell them at minimal cost. The carpet pads can be easily sanitized and reused. Beds, blankets, towels etc. can be placed over the mats for the maximum kitty comfort. Detailed instructions for disinfecting will be included in our Pampered Cats Cat Boarding Manual. You could also use blankets, towels and etc., but we found the laundry issue to be both time consuming and expensive due to drying costs, etc.

12. Padding Clips - Padding clips are used to hold pads on shelves. If they are not fastened, many cats will spend a considerable amount of energy redeploying them to suit their fancy – and many times the final resting place will be upside down in their litter box.

13. Roll-around Cart - We use a roll-around cart to place litter boxes on when scooping. Litter container and scoop disinfectant bucket are at opposite ends of the cart on the floor. As litter is scooped, the refuse is dropped into a plastic bag lined pail.

14. Litter Type - "Tidy Cat Clay Litter, Immediate Odor Control" has worked best for us from both odor control and cost points of view. Many of the inexpensive litters are terribly dusty, and when we saw the dust we would be breathing we were horrified. We never buy more than one bag of any litter we do decide to test until we see how it works in our kennel.

15. Cleaning Gloves - Cleaning gloves should be worn due to the potential impact of the disinfectants. We use disposable latex gloves for cleaning our units.

16. Medical Supplies -

A. Pill Poppers - Having a couple of different kinds and sizes on hand for pilling cats is important. Sticking fingers downs cats throats is best left to the vets.

B. Pill Crushers - These are available in most drug stores and crush pills to a powder that can be placed in a cat's wet food.

C. Latex Gloves - Also for handling meds, applying ointments, etc.

D. Pill pockets - Soft treats with holes in which you place the pill. We insert the pill in the pocket's hole and then knead the treat material over the open end to cover the pill. Then we hope our little friend will be duped into gobbling down the "kitty candy" before checking it out too closely. Most of them do. If they don't, we often try pressing two or three Temptations Cat Treats around the outside of the pill pocket. This approach will often succeed where the pill pocket alone fails.

17. Office Area - A small desk in the boarding area to process arrivals and departures, calculate bills, make notes on instructions for incoming cats, etc. is helpful. We have a four handset Panasonic 6.0 Digital Cordless Phone System that permits answering our business line in each of our private offices, our living area and the cat boarding office. Other standard office equipment will include a calculator, stapler, tape dispenser, computer, printer in addition to reservation pads, contracts and such.

18. Boarding Contract - We do have a boarding contract we use in special circumstances. We have not found it necessary to use contracts on a daily basis in our business in our area. This may not be the case for businesses located in other areas. Fortunately for us, we have never had a problem, but we are very conscientious and go the extra mile at all times on behalf of our owners and their pets.

All of the above information describes what works for us in running our business and is not intended as a specific recommendation for how and what you should do. You should check on all health and safety issues with your medical provider, and on all issues involving any kind of potential liability with your attorney.

CHAPTER 6

Catnap

"Flying Mackerel"

It was a sweltering summer day, and Carol and I were growing uncomfortable as we sat in our minivan outside the cargo building at Boston's Logan International Airport. Our good friend Mackerel, a tiger kitty that had stayed with us many times and of whom we were very fond, was the reason for our trip to the airport. Mackerel's mom and dad, like many New Englanders, had finally decided they would rather be in a warm climate during the winter and were moving to Florida. Due to the logistics of the move, Mackerel had to stay with us until he could be reunited with his owners at his new home in Florida.

Mackerel was a big tiger kitty that combined a fondness for calories with an aversion to physical activity. The result was a somewhat rotund physique and a propensity for making rather impressively sized contributions to his litter box.

Mackerel also loved to find spaces far too small for his robust figure and then dream up ways to wiggle into them. Often, removing him from these little spaces proved to be extremely difficult - especially when Mackerel did not cooperate, which was about 90% of the time. Little did we know that all Mackerel's foibles would merge together on this day to play an important role in what we call Mackerel's "Great Adventure."

Mackerel was scheduled to fly to his new home in Florida on Delta utilizing a service the airline called "Delta Dash." Pets were guaranteed to be off the plane and in your hands at the gate within thirty minutes of the plane's arrival. In summer, with temperatures often reaching 100+ degrees on the tarmac, such a service can be vital to a pet's health.

As things eventually worked out, the flight Mackerel was taking to Florida left on a Friday evening. Trying to make the best of things, I suggested to Carol that we make the 50 mile drive to Boston's Logan Airport, get Mackerel on his plane then we could go back to the city and go out to dinner. Little did I know how much I had underestimated the complications that could arise in getting one little kitty on an airplane.

Allowing plenty of time for the usual traffic delays in the city resulted in our arriving at the airport early when the expected delays were not encountered. This left us with about a two hour wait before departure, and since we could not bear to leave our little friend all alone in the cargo terminal, we sat in the car outside where Carol started to "think." When Carol starts to "think" it does not always bode well for me, as it often means I'm going to be doing something that nobody else in the world could get me to do. Little did I realize just how concerned my wife was about poor Mackerel's comfort.

"Well", she says, "It looks like it's time to start getting Mackerel ready to go."

"What's to get ready," I replied.

"You need to put the litter in the litter pan I put in the back of the van. It's been a long time since we left Plymouth. Mackerel may have to use the potty box before he gets on his plane."

"You have got to be kidding me. How are you going to get a cat to use the litter box in the car. He's going to think I've gone plumb crazy."

"Honey, will you please just put the litter in the litter box?"

I harbored severe doubt as to where this was all going. I began to become preoccupied with the thought that someone would see me trying to force this cat to use a litter box in the back of the minivan. Maybe I could talk my wife out of the whole idea, but then I remembered her slogan for a situation like this:

"A woman convinced against her will is of the same opinion still."

I had the sinking feeling that escaping from the potty box assignment was a remote possibility, at best.

Going around to the back of the minivan, I opened the trunk lid, took the potty box and poured the small bag of litter into the box. She always thinks of everything.

We cannot take a chance that Mackerel might escape in the airport, so down goes the trunk lid and into the back seat I lug my 240 pound six-foot two-inch frame. With Mackerel's carrier beside me on the back seat, I open the door, take him out and peacefully stroke his back. Little does the poor devil know that he is about to make feline history. I am sure that no human has ever attempted to assist him in using his potty box before. Picking Mackerel up I reach over the back seat and place him in the litter box. He looks up at with me with a funny, quizzical expression.

Carol, who's sitting comfortably in the front seat reading her book asks,

"How's it going. Honey?"

"Nothing yet. He just climbed out of the box."

"Well, put him back in. He'll get the idea."

"If you say so, darling."

After placing Mackerel in the liter box three or four times he began to tire of what he perceived as some kind of perverted game.

"He won't stay in the box. He doesn't want to use it."

"Well hold him in there for awhile."

Grasping Mackerel firmly, I place him in the box and hold him there. Now he starts to squirm in an attempt to get out, so I tighten my grip and Mackerel begins to sense this whole thing is going downhill fast. Obviously, in his opinion, the "cat man" had "lost it."

Mackerel, now fed up with the whole escapade, twisted and turned until I lost my grip on his big midriff. With feet spewing litter all over the back of the van he dove out of the box and towards the back seat. In a flash he flattened himself like a mouse going under a baseboard, disappearing under the back seat. If your familiar with the space under the seats in earlier minivans you know the odds against a quick extraction are now definitely weighted in Mackerel's favor.

We can't open any doors because the rascal might decide to go AWOL on the tarmac. This forces me to hang, sort of upside down over the back seat, peering into the miniscule cavity and trying to see my chubby little friend. As my eyes adjust to the light, way back in the corner, I can see two little eyes peering out. To make it even more interesting, Mackerel has puffed himself up like a blowfish. It's not going to be easy getting this raccoon shaped guy through a space that would turn a squirrel into a contortionist.

The inevitable queery from the front seat arrives.

"What's Mackerel doing now. Did I hear him scratching in the box."

"No, honey. That was Mackerel exploding out of the box. He's wedged under the back seat now and he's not coming out. How much time before his flight leaves?"

Now I'm afraid I'll have to remove the back seat with me in the car and no doors open so we can get Mackerel out of his hidey hole. Visions of that peaceful dinner, a walk along the waterfront are quickly fading into oblivion.

After giving Mackerel time to settle down, I figured I would try again. I could see the emergency services building a short distance away, and the thought occurred I may need to borrow their "jaws-of-life" before getting Mackerel out of his hole and on his plane.

Gaining access to my little buddy will first require climbing over the back seat into the rear cargo area of the minivan, no small feat for me. Falling over the back seat would be a better way to describe the process, and naturally various parts of me landed in that damnable potty box, tipping it and its remaining unsullied contents over the back floor of the van.

With a series of severe contortions I found I was able to get my hand and arm through the metal framework under the seat and just barely get my fingers on Mackerel. I gently stroked his back, slowly working my hand up to the nape of his neck as he started to purr. Scruffing him, I attempted to pull his body towards the opening through which we were going to have to compress that substantial physique.

With his head out from under the seat's frame, I worked my other hand in behind him and gently pushed with one hand while I pulled with the other. Pull and stretch, push and pull - ever so slowly and grudgingly Mackerel came back through the ridiculously tight space.

Once Mackerel was out I just held on for dear life and sat there, awash in litter, scratching his head and talking in low, soothing tones to keep the peace. One nice thing about cats is they can be very forgiving towards our ineptness. After a suitable interval, I opened the door of Mackerel's carrier, eased him into it, and shut the door.

"Did Mackerel do anything in his box?"

"*#@*@#%#@***@@@###" "Mackerel will be fine dear."(I've boarded cats that refused to pea or poop for three days out of sheer orneriness.)

Now behind schedule, we rushed off to the check in counter for animals where we found that numerous forms still had to be completed even though Mackerel already had his "ticket." No boarding passes and seat assignments preflight for kitties, that's for sure.

After completing all the work we were told to take Mackerel through the door and talk to the man in the animal holding room. After waiting what seemed an interminable amount of time a fellow arrived. After quickly scanning the paperwork he said,

"Just put him on top of those cases over there," pointing to two boxes that were about 5 foot square but only a foot or so in thickness.

"Wow, I said. "What's in there."

"Boa constrictors," he answered as he went down the hall, "Real big ones."

After all we had been through, we could not bear to walk out and just leave poor old Mackerel sitting on a pile of boa constrictors. I wondered if he could tell what was in those boxes. The boa constrictors were probably licking their chops, because Mackerel would sure make one tasty meal. Strong feelings of guilt prevented us from leaving Mackerel alone even though the boas were safely secured in the boxes.

We hung around the room until shortly before Mackerel's plane was loaded talking and assuring him that everything was going to work out ok. As long as there was not another nut on the plane with a potty box, I think Mackerel felt that he would do just fine.

Shortly after Flight 209 landed we received a call from Mackerel's mom. He had arrived clean as a whistle and none the worse for wear from the day's events.

We had now weathered another first in our life running a cathouse, and all of us seemed to have survived in pretty good shape.

The only sad aspect of the story is that we were never again to have the joy of Mackerel vacationing with us. We get very fond of our little friends in fur coats, and it is surprising how they stick in our memory. We will never forget our first "flying" kitty.

CHAPTER 7

OPERATING A KITTY B&B

REQUIREMENTS FOR BOARDING.

First and foremost is keeping both guests and caretakers safe. With cats, this primarily boils down to making sure guests have rabies and distemper shots and are spayed and neutered. Listening all night to a howling female kitty that's in heat is something one won't forget for a long time. Neutering for males is also critical, as unfixed males can introduce the foulest smelling odors into the guest house. And such odors can be difficult to eradicate.

Rabies shots are important for the B&B owner's protection. Many cats are allowed outside, and a bite from a rabies-infected animal could be percolating in an arriving cat and the owner might not even being aware of the situation.

The distemper shot (sometimes identified as FVRCP) protects the kitty against upper respiratory ailments and helps avoid the spread of that type of ailment in the B&B.

A reservation sheet of some type to keep the schedule organized is important. For a small home-based business like our own, keeping it simple has proved has proved adequate. Improvements can be made as things develop to meet the B&B's particular needs. Larger operations will want to expand the form to contain more information or move to a computerized reservation system so all staff members have sufficient information to do their jobs.

TAKING CARE OF CATS.

Some of the most important activities in our B&B are similar to those encountered in a people B&B:

1. Accommodations - Have the room all set up and add the cats bed (blanket, shirt, toys or whatever the owner brings from home) on arrival.

2. Food - Make sure cat has plenty of fresh water and a supply of dry food if applicable. Cats that have dry food usually have it available in the unit 24-7. Wet food is served two times a day.

3. Individual Care - One reason many people board is their pet is on medication. Some diabetic cats get insulin shots twice daily, others get thyroid medicine twice daily and so on. All cats are observed to make sure they are eating, drinking and using their potty box.

We always ask customers if they would like to have their cat be fed the same food they eat at home. This helps many cats end their "hunger strike" (a move designed to show the B&B owner who is really in charge) sooner rather than later. It also helps with cats that have digestive issues when fed certain types of food, something the B&B owner would not be aware of. Owner supplied food cuts down on food costs, but increases complexity of feeding if you have staff to deal with. Personally, I label all food and medicines when cats arrive, but find that I can commit all the details for the cats on food and medicine to memory. This would not work if you do not have an excellent memory or have to depend on staff to carry out feeding and med delivery activities.

ACTIVITIES

In case you have never noticed, cats are pretty good at entertaining themselves. Cats also exercise isometrically. Some cats will come out of their condo and spend time "introducing themselves" to the other cats, sometimes with hilarious results – other times they will get quite friendly with their neighbor. Many cats are quite happy sleeping in their condos and either will not come out, or will come out walk around a bit then go right back to their condo to take another nap.

We only allow cats out by family. We never let cats from separate families out together. There is always the risk of a fracas, or the increased potential for spreading one type or another of feline ailment. I know there are many places that do this, but we don't. The risks outweigh any possible benefit, and many customers are nervous about it.

WHAT DOES A TYPICAL DAY IN THE KITTY B & B LOOK LIKE?

Since my wife and I own and operate the B&B and have no employees, we are involved in every aspect of the operation.

Typically, our day starts about 8:00 am with cleaning and feeding. Each unit is cared for one at a time, so only one cat (or two or three if they are from the same family and in the same unit) are out of their condo at any given time. Each unit is cleaned, vacuumed and wiped down with disinfectant. Litter boxes are scooped, dry food dishes are refilled, wet food is served in plastic paper dishes and then the guest goes back into their unit as we move on to take care of the next "room." If any cats require medication, they are administered as we go. After cleaning and feeding activities are completed, we spend a few minutes checking on reservations and drop-offs and pick-ups scheduled for the day. These appointments are normally scheduled around 10:00 am or 4:00 to 5:00 pm to leave the middle portion of the day free for our own activities. Since cats do not require frequent care, as dogs do, we have more freedom than if we were boarding dogs, since dogs require more frequent walking to "take care of business." We are in and out of the boarding area during the day and give the cats attention as needed. Cats that would like to have some "out" time from their units can be let out (one family at a time) for a little R&R in the boarding area.

I find that I can typically care for 15-20 cats (cleaning and feeding) in about one and one-half hours. Boarding 15-20 cats a day at our present rate of $17.00 could generate between $255 – $340 per day, $1,785 – $2,380 per week, and $7,140 – $9,520 a month. - pretty good for running a home based kitty B&B. Although we have chosen not to operate at anywhere near that level, the potential is there to "grow the business."

DAY CARE

Day care is a big deal with dogs, as dogs need more attention throughout the day than cats do. Cats are extremely capable of going it alone for a day or two when needed.

In our opinion, day care service for cats is not practical. Having cats coming in and out morning and evening every day would dramatically increase the overhead costs of doing business. It also would be extremely stressful for the poor cat, and we would strongly recommend against it for both the cat's and innkeeper's sake. We have a two-day minimum stay to discourage any "day only" activity. There are situations where cats do needed to be boarded for one day only, such as when a home is being treated for insects, and we do perform that service, but we also stick to the two day minimum charge policy. As for day in and day out day care, we have only had one or two requests for such service in our 18 years of operation and have just politely declined.

SAMPLE FORMS

We use a simple spreadsheet type chart (see Appendix) to plan out our unit occupation schedule when we get busy to make sure we have a place for everybody. If you are running a larger business this probably won't work for you, and you may need to go with one of the computerized reservation systems. When you start however, the above will probably fit your needs for quite awhile.

CHAPTER 8

MARKETING, ADVERTISING AND PUBLIC RELATIONS

The term marketing includes all the activities involved in presenting a business to potential customers. We plan to cover a number of areas but will concentrate on activities that are relevant and affordable for small businesses.

POSITIONING YOUR BUSINESS

One marketing concept that will play a vital role in future success is called "positioning." What is positioning and why is it so important?

Positioning is the process of carving out in the customer's mind a unique "position" for a business relative to all the other products (read "other cat boarding alternatives") in the area. To illustrate, let's take a look at wristwatches, a product category with which we are all familiar.

When we hear the word "Rolex" we immediately think of a premier quality, very expensive watch – the ultimate in design and time-keeping performance. When you hear the word "Timex" a completely different picture springs to mind. Timex watches are inexpensive, tough timekeeping devices for those who want a utilitarian, reasonably priced watch. They "Take a licking and keep on ticking," thereby offering great value.

Each of the above positioning strategies have been developed over years of extensive marketing activities and include the advertising and publicity you see in various media channels. But in the beginning, each company had to make decisions about what kind of product they were going to offer and what kind of image they wanted to develop in the market. Creating a unique "position" in the mind of prospects in a market area regarding a business is what positioning is all about, and it is important.

There is a lot of buzz today about "branding." Personally, I think the concept is promoted heavily in the small business area to give so called branding experts leverage to convince you of the need need to hire them to help create your "brand." If you concentrate your efforts on positioning your business correctly, you will develop the image in the marketplace you need to succeed and in the process the whole branding issue will be resolved.

Now, how do we apply all this to opening a luxury B&B kitty boarding facility.

When we opened our business we knew we wanted to offer a boarding service for people who needed to have their kitties cared for while they were away from home. We also wanted to target people who cared deeply about their pets. But what position did we want to occupy in the mind of our target audience? Did we want to offer the lowest cost boarding option available or a luxury alternative offering exceptional physical accommodations with superb outdoor views and very involved caretakers.

We decided we wanted to position ourselves as a luxury feline Bed & Breakfast. Every decision we made subsequent to that point, even the choice of our business name was influenced by that positioning objective. This is a major reason positioning thinking should be done before a name is selected for the business.

NAMING A BUSINESS

When starting a new business, the playing field is wide open, and a name can be selected that fits well with the positioning objective. We chose the name Pampered Cats. When people board their cats they want to feel their kitty will be lovingly cared for, and the word "pampered" conveys that thought. We all like to be pampered, and the thought your kitty is being pampered while you're away helps assuage the guilt of leaving him/her behind. The name is simple, but it conveys a lot of meaning in two words.

The following example from my own experience can help illustrate the power of a name or phrase applied to a product. Back in the early 70's (19 not 18 in case you're wondering) the advertising agency I worked for was one of the fastest growing and highly regarded agencies in the eastern U.S. A major client, the Acushnet Company, manufactured Titelist golf balls. Market research showed that most golfers were impressed by what brands of equipment professional golfers chose to use on the tour. Research also showed that many of the leading pros on the tour were using the Titelist ball, and that these pros were winning more money than players using other balls. The agency decided to create a campaign emphasizing this winning record and positioning Titelist as "The Money Ball." The Titelist ball quickly became viewed in a whole new light – if you wanted to improve your game you probably would want to try the ball the pros were winning the most money with. Sales spiked as the message infiltrated the market.

A name can be a powerful tool. Choose your name carefully. You will be living with it for a long time.

LOGOTYPE

You will probably want to have a logotype for your business. It is a good idea to have one. It is also important to make sure that it contributes to the image you want to develop for your business.

Some logo designers will simply take the primary letters in your business name and make a fancy graphic out of it (the PC from Pampered Cats for example) and combine it with typography featuring the full company name. The major question to ask about any proposed logo is does the logo contribute to the image or market positioning objective for the business? Our final Pampered Cats logo was carefully designed and then refined through a number of sketches until we were satisfied that the name and graphic worked together to communicate the desired image.

The Pampered Cats logo features an illustration of a curled up kitty with a smug "I'm pampered" smirk on its face. We spent quite a bit of time fine tuning the drawing of the cat to achieve the desired effect. The curled up, contented looking kitty projected just the feeling we wanted to convey, and the words and the graphic work together to impart a powerful message. The Pampered Cat logo appears on marketing materials in the Appendix.

If you have artistic/design ability, or have a friend that does, you may be able to create your logotype using one of the many computer design programs available today. If you are not comfortable with that process, look at the logos of small businesses in your area and find out who designed them. Talk to the designer. A good designer will always want to know what you want your logo to communicate about the company. An Internet search for design firms and freelance artists in your area will uncover a number of sites showing work the various firms and individuals have done. Tell them what you can afford for a budget and ask what they could do for the amount you have to spend.

There are other more mundane aspects of the whole logo development process you should be familiar with. The logo should be produced in such a way that it will hold up when reduced to very small sizes, such as you might encounter on your business card or small newspaper ad.

Invest the time in your logo to perfect it so it will strengthen the image of the business in the market.

All of these activities, such as logo development, can require significant time and costs. This is one reason we plan to offer, if there is sufficient demand, ThePampered Cats Cat Boarding Manual. It will present a pre-packaged program that can be provided for those who wish to capitalize on an already proven program for improved results.

GRAND OPENING PUBLICITY

Preparing a news release (or story) to distribute to local media outlets when opening a business can be very effective in getting the news out. Media outlets will most often contact you for an interview with the objective of creating their own story. Newspapers, for example, will use the information in a release, but their reporter will craft the story to what they feel best fits the interests of their readers. A business editor at the local paper might present the story as an interesting business idea, while the pet reporter might take a completely different tack – but either way, the new business gets exposure – exposure most small businesses cannot afford to buy when just getting started. Just remember, the whole objective in the process is to get attention in the public eye for the business. Exactly how it is presented by the media is not something the business owner should try to manage. Media outlets may decide to kill the story if you interfere in the process.

You might find a local radio station interested in doing a story, or a local cable TV show might feature your facility on a pet program or animal enthusiast show. The bottom line is getting the story/news release out on as wide a basis as possible and then taking advantage of any interest you can generate with strong follow up.

The news release we wrote for our facility on opening resulted in stories being done by a number of newspapers in our market area. After receiving the release, the editor called and came for a visit and interview along with a photographer to take some photos and write the article shown. Text in news releases should be either one and one-half or double spaced when sent to media. Full details on all these items will be provided in the Pampered Cats Cat Boarding Manual.

MEDIA ADVERTISING

A small business can go broke real fast spending too much money on advertising. As one advertising legend put it, "I know half of my advertising budget is wasted, but the only problem is I don't know which half." Achieving success in a boarding business is a marathon, not a sprint. Pampered Cats has limited its print advertising expenditures to one monthly small space ad in the local Pet Gazette newspaper and a monthly appearance in the major area newspaper's Pet Section.

INTERNET

Our website has been, hands down, the major new business generation tool for our business. With my advertising and creative writing background, we were well suited to the task of developing a web site that really connects with cat lovers. The site creates an image of a warm, homey place that is operated by people who are cat lovers themselves and who care for visitor's cats just as they do for their own.

You will need to create a good website if you are going to succeed, because today the Internet is where the action is. Just about nobody uses the Yellow Pages anymore. You want to make sure you are listed in the Yellow Pages directory, but paying for an ad is pretty much a waste of money. The one exception to this rule could be your start-up year, when you need every bit of exposure you can get. Our experience is that 90% of people looking for a cat boarding facility start right out with an Internet search. Your site needs to create an image that will separate you from the competition and make you appear to be the most desirable facility. Many prospective customers will want to come for a personal visit after they find you on the Internet, so make sure you welcome pre-boarding visits. It is the final link in closing the deal.

The Pampered Cats Cat Boarding Manual will provide more detailed information on this subject describe a way to include your business on a high quality web site that capitalizes on our 18 years of professional marketing experience and search engine exposure, thus providing you with an Internet presence right from the start with very little work on your part.

SPHERES OF INFLUENCE

Veterinarians – You will want to get around and visit all the veterinary practices in your area and present your new facility to anyone that will listen. Ask if you can leave brochures and cards for their customers that might be in need of your services. If you get a vet who seems to take a liking to you ask him/her if they could "mentor" you if you should have any medical issues arise with your guest kitties. Veterinarians that are just starting their own practice are good ones to ask about this because they sometimes have a bit more time to help someone else out. Just make sure to call only when you need help. Don't make a nuisance out of yourself and be sure to send any referrals you can to your "mentor" vet and tell the customer you are referring to mention your name.

Pet Stores – Talk to employees of the pet stores in your area about what you are doing. Ask if you can leave brochures and cards. Most of the larger chains can't accommodate this, but many independent stores can and will.

Animal Rescue Shelters – Let people know at the shelter/rescue organizations about your new business. If you can volunteer at the shelter you will make new acquaintances in the field. You will meet lots of people who will have to board their kitty someday and will know that you exist. If you can afford to donate to help support rescue/shelter organizations financially, do so. The kitty volunteers will spread the word.

Customers – Do everything you can to please every customer and every prospective customer. Go the extra mile all the time. Bend over backwards, never complain, thank everybody, and tell them stories about their kitties antics while they were with you.

You will be appreciated and loved. This is a very personal service business. I carry all the ladies cats out to the car for them. Even those who do not need it appreciate the courtesy. I carry cats out to the car for anybody that excepts my offer to do so. I tell them it's my way of saying goodbye to my new kitty friend so they don't feel self-conscious. I enjoy helping people and they enjoy being helped. Do everything you can for their cats. You are in a position to see some things owners may miss at home, especially if they let their cats go outside (more details in the Pampered Cats Cat Boarding Manual). But be sure to be genuine – people can spot a fake a mile away – especially when it concerns family, and believe me, these little friends in fur coats are family to your customers. Treat every prospect with the same care and enthusiasm you treat your customers. If you do, your customers will refer their friends to you, they will say good things to the vets and other animal care people in the area and help your business grow. Always remember, cat people are great people. I don't think you will ever find a greater group of people to serve.

Business Card Technique – I don't know where I read about this one, but it has worked very well for us and was a big help early on when we could use all the business we could possibly generate. The idea is this: when you give your business and money to someone in your community, make sure they get your business card along with your money. Your local restaurant, donut shop, convenience store… you know the drill. Give or leave a card everywhere you go. It works. If your buying clothes at Macy's, the clerk who rings you up gets a card plus a "Yeah, we run a luxury Bed and Breakfast for cats. Do you have a cat?" It's a sure conversation starter, and I can assure you that we turned quite a few of those people into very happy customers. Even people who don't have a cat will often say, "My sister has a cat and was looking for someplace to board her." Or, "My mother is going on vacation and she might need to get her kitty taken care of while she is gone." I even hook telemarketers calling in to our business that will ask, to be polite, what we do. The answer, "We run a Bed & Breakfast for cats." The reply, "What's that?" Off you go on your story. I talked to one Verizon operator trying to sell us a phone upgrade for at least 5 minutes about cats and what we do before she remembered what she was supposed to be doing – selling us. This is a fun business and people will get interested easily because there is no real pressure on them to make a commitment or spend their money. Talk to everybody. When we were buying the materials to build our condos the forklift operator at Home Depot asked if he could help us.

"And what are you doing with the melamine panels, he asked?"

"We're building cat condos"

"What's that?"

So we were off to the races and gave him the whole Bed & Breakfast story. Turns out this hulking guy pushing around the pallets on the forklift had two or three cats and a real soft spot for his kitties. You just never know when you will strike pay dirt by starting a conversation.

Everywhere you go, give out cards to anybody who will talk. People get a kick out of the whole idea and you'll get into a lot of very nice conversations with nice people. Cat owners are the greatest people you could ever want to meet. And make sure you have brochures that you can leave with the vets, pet stores, groomers and so on.

Be friendly, and as you gain experience you can offer people help with issues they may be having with their cat. They will ask you all sorts of questions and that is one the best new business practices you can develop.

Working with Customers and Potential Customers – If you do a good job marketing your business, you will find prospective customers tend to fit into two categories. The first consists of those who call or email and make a reservation. Many of these prospects will have heard good things about your business from local vets, friends, and other people who have boarded with you.

The second category consists of those who want to come and take a tour of your facility and meet you in person. If you are good at working with people, you will readily sense that these individuals are very carefully trying to size you up to see if they believe you are actually the caring, loving person you claim to be in your marketing efforts.

You need to be patient with these prospects. Oftentimes telling them stories about cats that have visited with you, asking questions about their pet and getting to know them personally is far more productive than just being "business-like efficient," thereby communicating the feeling you are in a hurry to get on to the next thing on your agenda. Spend the time and you will make a customer, a friend, and a long time patron if you deliver on your promises.

Always remember, kitty boarding is a service business. Accommodating customer needs in everything from their cat's individual needs to difficult travel schedules and resulting drop off and pick up times can be a pain, but those appreciative customers will become very loyal to your business for the trouble you go to.

CHAPTER 9

COMPUTERS

You could run your B&B today without owning a computer – although I would not recommend it. Computers can save you a lot of time even if you are only using them for the more mundane tasks of running your life and business.

Here are a few areas where computers can help operate more professionally and efficiently:

- Information acquisition via the internet for business planning and operation.
- Financial record keeping.
- Bill paying for family and business
- Reservation systems
- Creation of marketing tools
- Building a customer database
- Email communications
- Promotion via the Internet
- Web site marketing
- Tax preparation and filing

There are more for sure, but the above list includes many of the important ones.

Once a decision is made to utilize a computer a choice must be made between the two major platforms available – Windows PC and Macintosh.

I have used both platforms and prefer the Mac over various brands operating on Windows. My experience has been the PC is far more susceptible to system software problems that require professional assistance (that means you pay $100 or more an hour) to resolve the issues. The problem has nothing to do with the various brands of computers themselves, but more with the PC operating system. If you are familiar with the technical issues, such as those that PCs often have with registry files, for example, and know how to fix them, then you will be fine with a PC. If you're like me, and have little patience for fiddling with technical issues, and you just want the darn thing to work so you can keep operating, it is my opinion you will be much happier in the long run with a Mac.

Now, someone is going to tell you that the Mac is a lot more expensive and it won't run PC programs, some of which you will want for your business. The Mac is more expensive, and the old adage "you get what you pay for," holds true here as it does with many other products. When your system is down and you can't get the help you need to get back up and running again you will wish you went with a Mac. And the Mac CAN run PC software. This is accomplished with programs like Fusion and Parallels that actually let you run both Windows and Mac programs simultaneously on the same computer and on the same desktop. These programs basically create a Windows Operating System computer on your Mac. They accomplish this by creating an emulation hard drive, that is, for all intents and purposes, a PC. If the Windows emulated "drive" on your computer catches a cold, you can simply throw it in the trash and restore it from the BACKUP you will have made to prepare for such a situation. Whatever system you use, always have a backup! If you are using reservation software you better backup daily. This can be easily accomplished using SuperDuper or Carbon Copy Cloner on the Mac, backup programs that make incremental backups so you don't have to wait while the whole hard drive is backed up file by file each time you backup. Only the files that have changed since the last backup have to be processed and saved.

Fusion and Parallels are available for around $100.00 or so and give you the option of having the best of both PC and Mac worlds available to you on one computer. You do also have to buy a copy of Windows to install under Fusion. In my experience (and other users I know) Fusion is probably the best option.

Now, you might say why go to all this bother. Here's why I decided to go this route.

Even though my wife was a COBOL programmer, she had no interest in the technical operations of the PC operating system. She had one PC at home that was constantly freezing to the "blue screen of death" most PC users are familiar with. My son runs a technical computer service business, and PCs and their problems have kept him well employed for a number of years. I spent hundreds of dollars getting him to fix the old PC, always figuring this would be the last time – but the last time never arrived. Finally, enough was enough, and I took my wife to the Mac store and said, "You are getting a shiny new Mac computer." That was the end of the problems and she has been working away on her Macs (she now has two Mac desktops and a laptop) and loves them just as much as I love mine. I have always been able to resolve any issues that have arisen on both of our machines even though I am not what you would call a "techie." Generally speaking, Windows has been more susceptible to viruses and malware that can raise havoc with your computer than the Mac OS.

The temptation is great to rationalize, thinking to yourself that "The Mac is more expensive and I want to save money." My advice is to spend the money on the Mac. Buy a used Mac if necessary. Refurbished Macs are available at MacMall and other suppliers. Small Dog Electronics in NH and Other World Computing aresources for acquiring a pre-owned, refurbished Mac. You really won't save money buying a PC because you are going to spend a lot more money getting your PC fixed when things go awry.

Although the new Windows platform releases have improved from a reliability standpoint, I still cannot get over the problems we ran into and the frustration endured when I had to wait for my son to get the time to get to our office and fix the computer so both my wife and I could get back into operation and be productive again.

BANKING

It was not too long ago I finally gave up on writing and mailing checks out to pay my bills. I liked that old feeling of having my canceled checks in hand – proof I had fulfilled my obligations. When I began to realize how much time it was taking me to write out the pile of checks, address the envelopes, then pay close to $.50 per envelope to get them to get them mailed, I knew I had to make some changes. Old things feel familiar and comfortable, but in today's busy world sometimes those things just gotta go. The time had come and I realized I just had to change.

Wow! With on-line banking I was paying the bills for both business and household in just a few minutes each month. If I am really busy, I just send people what I know I roughly owe them, or even the same amount I payed the previous month, and that usually keeps everyone happy.

Today, most on-line accounts enable you to export your transactions to spreadsheet or data files so you can enter them into Quicken, for example, or other similar programs for financial management and tax return purposes.

RESERVATION SYSTEMS

The size of the business is going to influence the decision as to whether one should utilize a computerized reservation system.

We have always operated our business on a manual basis using paper reservation forms we fill out when the reservation is made via phone or Internet. When we are extremely busy, we make out a "spreadsheet" type boarding schedule to maintain control and make adjustments as needed. This works well for us because we run the business as a husband and wife team and do not have any communication issues to deal with regarding staff.

We have thought from about building our own simple database reservation system utilizing software such as FileMaker Pro. To date we have not found the anticipated benefits to be sufficient to go to the work or and expense of building such a system.

When running a large operation, however, where staff will be involved in running the business, you are almost assuredly going to need a reservation system to maintain control since a number of people will be involved in taking reservations. This effort will have the side benefit of simultaneously generating a customer database.

INFORMATION ACQUISITION

When you first get started on planning for your business you will be looking to assemble information on a number of subjects. Assembling the information quickly and efficiently will require the use of a computer with access to the Internet.

Much helpful information in operating the business is available on the Internet. Questions regarding feline health issues is a good example. Searching such a phrase as "heavy feline urination" will provide information on the various physical ailments that can cause cats to urinate excessively. Advising customers of any issues noticed can be important. If the cat is an outside cat, for example, the owners may have no idea the cat is urinating excessively because the cat does not use an inside litter box. In any case, at least discuss the situation with your customer. They will appreciate your concern.

As is the case with most business operations, from time to time, you will find yourself requiring access to information at the most inconvenient times – like late at night when a cat is manifesting troubling symptoms and you can't call your favorite veterinarian for advice. There is also the matter of education, as it is incumbent on you to learn all you can about feline matters, including behavioral and medical issues, medications, etc.

You will also find there is much valuable information available on general business subjects. Everything from Small Business Loans (from the Small Business Administration, a government entity) and local loan sources, state and federal taxation, insurance, interest rates and education courses and programs to name a few.

The computer is a tremendous asset to the operation of even the smallest business. For starters, download OpenOffice, available free of charge at OpenOffice.org. It provides all the capability of that big, expensive office program sold by you know who.

THE COMPUTER AS A MARKETING TOOL

The computer has become an invaluable weapon in the marketing arsenal of large and small businesses. We will take a look in the following pages at some of the most important areas in which computers can help build a thriving, successful business.

YOUR WEBSITE

Creating a good web presence is critical to the success of any business today. More than 90% of our new business of our new clients come from our website because the web is the first place people look when they need to board their feline buddy. We get listed in the local Yellow Pages due to our business phone line, but paying for an ad, at least in my opinion and in my area, is a waste of money.

Marketing money and effort is better put into your web presence. That is where the action and the money is. We'll discuss the various aspects of what makes a good website in considerably more detail in following pages.

WEBSITE, EMAIL AND RESERVATIONS

Your website will generate requests for information and reservations. Many people will email through the website. Others will call after viewing the site. Email has increasingly become a preferred method of communication for a number of reasons. Convenience for both parties is a major contributing factor. Often we get email from people we can see sent the email during the night. Possibly they visited our site late and wanted to get the process started when it was certainly not a good time to use the phone. We reply the minute we see the email so they have an answer when they next check their mail.

Recently we received an email from Kenya requesting information about our facility and asking for answers to a number of detailed questions. The cats were coming from Nairobi through Heathrow in London and then on to Boston. The owners would not be available to pick them up in Boston and wanted to know if we could pick them up, take them to our B&B and board them for a month during the customer's move from Africa to the Midwestern U.S.

Answering their questions and getting them to feel comfortable with both our facility and ourselves personally was all accomplished in a series of emails. The kitties eventually arrived and thirty days later were picked up and headed off to their new home.

Since I am a writer by profession, that skill helps me communicate effectively with people and establish a bond even in the absence of face-to-face or telephone conversation. But, if you truly seek to serve your clients and assist them through the harrowing trauma of their kitty-separation anxiety, that will come through as you work on developing your written communication skills.

CREATING YOUR WEB SITE

You have a number of options available to you for creating your website. We will review the alternatives.

1. Hire A Web Design Company To Create Your Site.

Web design companies are typically oriented to creating web sites using text and photographs supplied by the customer. If you need the text for your site written, you will probably need to hire a writer to accomplish that task. Most web design outfits are pretty good at finding photos to use on your site. The key here is to make sure the web people understand your business and the image you desire to project.

2. Create Your Website Yourself.

There is software available on the market that makes it relatively easy to build a simple web site. With any such software you will face somewhat of a learning curve. The learning curve for simpler programs, however, is nothing compared to the effort required to master a professional level program like Dreamweaver. Many web hosting companies, such as Go Daddy, have packages that will enable you to build and host a basic web site and have it up and running very quickly.

3. Hire A "Total Package" Website Development Firm.

These firms offer the marketing, copywriting, graphic design and website production skills to create the whole web package. My marketing and writing background, for example, includes creating websites for small to medium sized companies in a variety of industries and typically cost $2,000 – $3,000 for a site of 4-6 pages. This includes starting from scratch, analyzing the business, suggesting a marketing approach, writing the text, designing and producing pages. Also included is keyword selection and implementation to maintain as high a profile as possible in the search engines, a process referred to as Search Engine Optimization (SEO).

If you are comfortable with computers, you can take on as much or as little of the process as you feel comfortable with.

We hope to help start-up kitty B&Bs through our Pampered Cats Cat Boarding Manual program tying new B&Bs into our own site to take advantage of our Search Engine Rankings. This approach will help a new business save time and effort during the startup process.

CREATING OTHER MARKETING TOOLS

Your business is going to need brochures, flyers, business cards, letterheads, reservation forms, client agreements envelopes, labels small ads, vehicle signs and more. You can create some of these materials in a word processor, but the word processor leaves a lot to be desired from a finesse point of view.

I use Adobe InDesign for my business, but I have years of experience with InDesign and its predecessor, Adobe PageMaker. InDesign is an extremely powerful program, but it also has a steep learning curve and is quite expensive. If you have a good sense of design, you may find a free program like Scribus (or similar program) will work for you. You may also need a drawing program similar to Adobe Illustrator, another complex and expensive program, but the free Draw portion of Open Office may meet your needs. EazyDraw is another good program to take a look at. Otherwise just do an Internet search for "free drawing programs." A simple photo manipulation program would probably meet your needs as opposed to the state-of-the-art Photoshop program from Adobe. If you are not artistic, you may find that hiring a local artist to develop the "artwork" you require to be cost effective and a time saver for preparing the physical items mentioned above. The artwork can be provided to you in computerized form so you can make changes and output art or files for use with suppliers as needed. Most of the suppliers you will work with will accept computer files such as PDF, TIFF, JPEG, EPS, GIFF and others to print or produce the items you require.

By utilizing a reasonably priced Pampered Cats Program contained in our manual you may find that you can save substantial time and money, since all of the items you need to get started can be obtained with minimal effort on your part. You will be very busy getting your physical facility designed, built and ready for guests and don't want to be delayed and frustrated dealing with tasks with which you are not familiar.

OTHER WEB TOOLS

As you get started, the social media sites can also be used to draw attention to your business and open the lines of communication with potential customers. Blogs can be very effective if you are a good communicator and willing to spend the time it takes to write and manage a good blog. Facebook is becoming an increasing popular channel for communicating with target audiences. YouTube can also help draw traffic to your web site if you can create cat videos that are either funny or informative.

We have not used social media to date because we have not needed to generate more business than we currently have. That may change as competition increases and we have to be more active in these venues to maintain our business volume.

CUSTOMER DATABASE

One advantage of a Reservation/Customer Database program is the ability to keep notes on customer preferences and cat issues, such as aggressive behavior, medical/health issues, medications, food preferences, cats' veterinarian information, etc. Even a simple database program could easily be used to build a customer database.

CHAPTER 10

CATNAP

"Sugar High"

"Joe, Duke has become diabetic and I have to board him from the 18th thru the 25th of the month. I want Duke to stay with you. I know you don't give insulin shots, but that's not a problem, because I'm going to come down and train you how to give the shots. Remember, I'm a nurse, don't worry, it'll be a piece of cake."

I realized Candy was paying us a compliment, and I had grown rather fond of Duke, who was a bit like a grouchy old man that's always giving you a hard time, but who, for some reason, you still have a soft spot in your heart for. And then there was the fact that I really didn't want my old pal Duke going someplace else.

Duke had stayed with us a number of times before he became diabetic. He was a handsome orange and white cat with an extensive repertoire of boarding antics – some intimidating, some funny. He would hiss, spit, growl, and at times, lurch toward the condo door in attack mode with paw upraised as we passed by. He would normally harass us like this for a couple of days before he would relax and become semi-civilized. By the end of his stay he had usually warmed up and would deal with us in a much less hostile manner.

On his first stay with us, Duke's behavior when Cindy came to pick him up was hilarious. Duke was comfortably stretched out on the floor of his condo on Candy's arrival. When he spotted her, he whirled, turning his back to her, and thrusting his head in the corner of his condo. It was obvious he was going to play the guilt card to the max. It is sort of comical, but we see this behavior quite frequently.

Kneeling down, Candy spoke quietly and opened the door. Duke responded by spinning around, snarling and spitting like he was going to tear mom to pieces. Second and third attempts to greet Duke met the same fate.

Deciding enough was enough, I put on the gloves and removed Duke from his unit, enduring his hissing, spitting, and mad flailing of all four paws while I eased him into his carrier. Sometimes it looks to owners like their kitty is so happy at the Inn that they just don't want to leave.

A number of visits had left Duke's antics indelibly imprinted in our minds, and he was definitely not on our "short list" of cats on whom we desired to be trained to give insulin shots.

We had not been boarding diabetic cats since the inception of our business because of our discomfort with the idea of giving shots and fear of potential problems. Often, when cats are boarded, they will be "thrown off their feed," sometimes refusing to eat for a couple of days. For most cats this is not a problem. As long as they use their litter box we know they are fine and when they get hungry they eat.

With a diabetic cat however, this can be a problem. Cats need to eat when they are receiving insulin shots. We were concerned about the eating issue and for that reason had decided to decline boarding diabetic cats.

Carol had also been hesitant about giving insulin shots from the beginning, a fact she continued to impress on me with repeated assertions as to her lack of desire to become what she viewed as a feline paramedic.

As luck would have it, Carol was not around when Candy called. During our conversation I couldn't help but think of how much we liked both Candy and Duke. The result was I eventually blurted out, "Yes, Candy, we can do that."

As soon as I hung up my mind began to race as to how I would explain the expansion of our business into feline health care to Carol. My solution, like all good solutions, was simple.

"Don't worry, I'll do it if you won't."

Little did I know the baptism of fire Duke was going to give us in the art of giving insulin shots. I have always been grateful to him, though, because like a really demanding coach, Duke taught us well. We have only had one or two cats in the last 18 years that were so wild that giving them a shot was not safe for us.

The date of Duke's first visit since becoming diabetic came and Candy arrived at the appointed time. She smoothly slid Duke out of his carrier with the proficiency that nurses have in such matters, grasped him in the manner he was accustomed to, slipped the needle in, and it was over before we could blink. I think what had happened was she had shot the old grouch in the butt with his insulin before he even knew what was happening in all the confusion of getting into his new room at the "cat house."

"See, nothing to it," Candy smiled.

Well, it did look pretty easy the way Candy did it, so we figured we could probably handle it.

That evening, as we served supper to our guests, we finally arrived at old Duke's unit.

Opening the door and reaching for Duke, I was greeted with a repertoire of histrionics that was quite amazing. He whirled to face me as he hissed, snarled and spit – all in one symphonic movement – and made a couple of passes at me with both front paws flailing away in rapid succession.

I slammed the door in horror and made a quick retreat, bumping into Carol, needle at the ready, with a truly sick look on her face.

There is something about a screaming, hissing, growling, spitting, "kaacking" cat that sends chills down your spine and makes your hair stand on end. No matter how many times you hear it, you still get a jolt when you haven't heard it for a while.

Regaining our composure, we started to analyze just how we were going to get the needle inserted into this ferocious beast that was working on doing a terrific impression of the feline hero in the movie "Mouse Hunt."

On went the protective gloves. As we approached Duke's condo again. He knew exactly what was up and went through the whole kicking and screaming process all over again, but this time to no avail. Opening the door I surprised Duke with my slight of hand, swooping him out and onto the desk. Duke didn't miss a beat though. He kept right on hissing, spitting, growling and terrifying my poor wife who was trying, ever so quietly, to sneak up on his right flank. At this point our old buddy realized he was still doing a pretty good job playing the intimidation game. I made the mistake of letting up ever so slightly on my grip, giving Duke that little bit of space he needed for his next maneuver. As Carol's hand touched his backside he kaacked, spat and spun his head around in one lightening move that almost got his teeth to Carol's hand.

This may have been the pinnacle of our story with Duke. My hands are full of enraged cat and my "medic" is not sure if I am capable of holding the cat down or not, resulting in a case of shaking hands and my worrying if the needle has as much chance of hitting me as it does Duke.

In the next skirmish I take firm hold of the torso and try to get Carol to come in for the kill. Each time she touches Duke's backside though, he erupts in a frenzy of writhing and twisting in an attempt to get at Carol's hand. I adjust my grip so the protective gloves are between Duke's teeth and Carol's hand no matter how hard he twists and pulls. After another couple of aborted passes Duke was finally pierced and medicated. Carefully lifting him off the table I placed him back in his unit. As my grip eased he twisted, and lunged for my arm with a growl that sounded more like a rottweiler than a pussycat.

Luckily, Duke has a good appetite, so we never had to worry about him not eating. And he was smart enough to know that medication is always followed by a gourmet meal tailored to his preferences to make sure he would eat.

I didn't look forward to opening the condo door again immediately after his shot, so we fed a couple of other cats before returning to serve up Duke's meal. As I approached Duke was sitting as calm as can be behind the screened door with what I would call a smirk on his face. He almost looked like he was smiling! As I opened the door and lowered the food tray he surged towards my hand before I could react and started rubbing his head up and down my arm , purring away as he sniffed his supper approvingly.

Every single day Duke has stayed with us since we have repeated this procedure twice daily. I finally came to believe it was all a big game for Duke from which he achieved some sort of feline satisfaction. It seemed at times as if he was taking upon himself the responsibility of teaching us not only how to give insulin shots, but to personally make sure that we would be forever prepared to deal with the most impossible of patients.

I have to admit, Duke, you did a good job.

Duke and Candy will always have a special place in our hearts. They prepared us well for caring for cats that don't like shots.

Epilog

Duke had failed noticeably the last time that he was with us. A short time later Candy called.

It turned out Duke was having a lot of difficulty walking and even getting in and out of his litter box. Candy's husband Mark decided it was unfair to let him suffer any longer and had taken him to the vet to be released from his trial by entering into the restful sleep of eternity. Candy cried as she told us about the difficulties Duke had experienced in the end, and we have always taken it as a great compliment that she would think to call us at such a time. I think she knew that we were as fond of Duke as anybody outside their family could be.

CHAPTER 11

POLICIES

The policies we will be discussing here are limited specifically to the cat care aspects of operating a boarding business. If you are going to employ staff, you will have need for additional policies specific to employer/employee relations we have not attempted to cover. Employee policies and governmental regulations should be dealt with by consultants familiar with those issues. As with all our discussions, we tell you what has worked for us in our business, but every company is different and our policies and strategies may not be suited to your particular situation, You should seek the assistance of a professional where required.

ADMISSION RULES

We do not accept cats that are not up to date on their shots – and this is especially important in the early stages of the business. There will be some exceptions to this issue down the road, but in the beginning it is far better to insist on cats being up to date on vaccinations.

Cats should have feline distemper (frequently listed as FVRCP) and rabies shots (Merial PureVax vaccine etc).

From the feline innkeeper's perspective, the primary reason for the distemper shot is it protects cats against what is commonly referred to as "upper respiratory infections" and "kennel cough." These terms refer to respiratory infections that are somewhat similar to the flu contracted by humans. The FVRCP shot works much like a human flu shot, helping the cat's body to build antibodies that protect against the disease. Symptoms exhibited when a cat is coming down with URI include sneezing, coughing, runny eyes, runny nose, difficulty breathing, etc. If a cat arrives with any of these symptoms, check with the customer's vet before accepting the cat, as a cat could have allergy problems that would explain the symptoms. We have encountered cats with allergies, but we assume the cat is sick until proven otherwise. Any cat manifesting the above symptoms is immediately isolated from the general boarding population to protect the other cats. Upper respiratory infections spread like wildfire in a boarding kennel. The virus is quickly transmitted via airborne particles from sneezing and coughing, by animal to animal contact, and by being transmitted from caretakers hands and clothing. It is actually worse than the "kids in kindergarten syndrome."

Many vets no longer give FVRCP shots to cats older than ten years of age if they have had the shots up until that age. The reason is cats have usually built up the maximum amount of immunity to the disease by that point, and further injections do not provide any increased protection. This exception can require some vigilance as to making sure the cat did get the shots earlier in life.

We often run into situations where a caller says, "my cat doesn't need the shot because it is an inside cat." We won't board a cat over ten years of age if it has not had the FVRCP shots previously. If a cat did not get the earlier shots, it should be vaccinated, hopefully a few weeks before it arrives at your facility, allowing time for the immune system to process the vaccine and build up resistance. Getting the shot the day before the cat arrives is NO good. If the cat only had a couple of shots in the first few years and none since then, we require the cat to have the shot to protect ourselves. And, as previously mentioned, the cat should have the shot as far in advance of the time it will be boarding as possible. If the cat had the shots for 8 or 9 years – even four or five – we would board the cat, as that number of shots usually provides sufficient protection.

Rabies shots are a complete necessity for any cat that goes outside. Most people realize this and we run into very few outside cats that have not had their rabies shot. Some people with cats that are never allowed outside will not bother with the rabies shot. We advise those people to get the shot anyhow, since it is always possible for an inside cat to escape from the house in some sort of emergency situation or by mistake. If an inside cat has not been outside and does not have any unidentified bites or scratches, we accept them. If such a cat arrives and we find it has a bite or scratch, we immediately institute full precautionary measures in handling the kitty. Sometimes, for example, the bite may come from another cat in the household and may not be a risk, but innkeepers can't afford to take a chance. If the cat needs to be handled, we use protective gloves, and if the cat is aggressive in any way, we take all necessary measures to protect ourselves against a bite from the kitty.

Leukemia shots have been found to be linked to the occurrence of tumors at the vaccine's injection site and many vets now recommend against giving these shots. We have never had a problem with a case of Leukemia (HIV) transfer at our facility. Vets will tell you that the virus is fairly fragile once outside the body, and does not remain in an active state for very long. We have boarded cats that are HIV positive, but the cat is isolated from the boarding room and separate tools and supplies are used to protect against any transfer in spite of the relatively low risk of transmittal.

Ringworm is another malady to watch for. We closely observe the fur coat of boarders for any ring-like bare spots that expose a patch of skin. This is symptomatic of ringworm infection, a very contagious affliction. It is usually only encountered with outside cats or cats with exposure to outside cats, such as where one cat goes outside and the other does not. Other pets that go outdoors can also import the ailment. If you see the ring-like bare-spot symptom, contact the cat's vet immediately to see if they are aware of the situation. It is possible it may be an allergy or even an old wound. Some allergies can also present symptoms similar to ringworm.

We make sure cats are spayed and neutered. Listening to a howling female kitty in heat all night long is something you won't forget for a long time. Neutering for males is critical, as unfixed gents can introduce the foulest smelling odors into the guest house – and believe me, the odor can be very difficult to eradicate. We learned that lesson when we had a couple from Russia come to board their kitties. The fact their male cats were not neutered slipped through the cracks somehow. Evidently they don't neuter the males in Russia to the extent we do here in the U.S. It took us weeks to get the sickish sweet smell of their spraying out of the B&B.

LENGTH OF STAY

Most people are looking to board their cats for vacations, business trips and the like. These stays range anywhere from a few days to a month or more. People involved in real estate transactions and relocating to another area can sometimes require two months or longer due to complications in selling one house and closing on another.

We have had cats boarding with us anywhere from a couple of months up to as long as two years – although the two year stay was a rare exception.

We get a call every once in awhile from someone who only wants to board their cat for one night (or possibly two). The "wary" antenna goes up as soon as we hear the stay will be so short. If it is an existing customer it is no problem, but if it is a new customer, we want to know the reason why they only want to board their cat for one or two nights. There are a few valid reasons, one being that they are having the house fumigated or bombed for fleas and need to get the cat out of the house for 24 hours. But, if there does not seem to be a believable reason for such a short stay we are very careful, because this is one of the ploys people use when they are trying to abandon a cat.

Here's is an example of a recent call we received. On answering the phone the caller says,

"I want to board my cat."

"OK, do you have the kitty's shot records."

"No, we're moving and we have them all packed away."

"OK, how long do you need to board your cat for," I reply.

"Just overnight."

"That's a pretty short stay, how come."

"I just need to get her out of the house"

"Well, when do you want to drop her off," I answer

"Right now."

"Ouch, not much notice. How long will it take you to get here?"

"Like I say, right now, I'm parked in your driveway."

"I'm terribly sorry, but I can't fit your kitty in on such short notice. Hopefully we can help you out the next time you have a need."

There was no way this individual was ever going to return to get the cat. He displayed just about every conceivable sign of a person attempting to abandon their cat. Although this is an extreme example, for sure, we are very careful in such situations as we do not currently need another family cat.

We have a two day minimum stay, and even if the cat is only here one day we charge for two days. It takes work to get ready for the cat, consumes supplies to outfit the unit, then more work to clean up after the cat leaves. I know I should make the minimum more, but we are a service organization and I try to keep things affordable for the many people that don't have a lot of extra money.

On longer stays, over a month, we provide a discounted rate. This helps customers ease the pain a bit for boarding their cat.

CHILDREN IN THE CAT HOUSE

A few comments here about children in the cat house. We make absolutely no recommendations on the subject. You must make and follow your own policies and ask your attorney regarding liability. We only tell you what we do and how it has worked for us.

The only reason we address the subject is that some of you that may be contemplating running a kitty B&B have children and will have to deal with the issue. It is much like running a farm and allowing the children to help with the animals. Safety comes first, but children do learn to become responsible adults by caring for God's little creatures.

Most children are fascinated by the cats. We allow customers to bring their children when they drop off and pick up their cats because the event is such a big deal to many of the children, but we keep a very close watch on them while they are here. We make sure they do not touch any cats, create excess noise or whatever. You should clear things like this with your legal counsel just to avoid potential issues.

Most of my foster children and grandchildren love the cats and pester me to death to help out taking care of the kitties. We lay down a number of rules they have to follow and they know if they violate any rules they will be banished from the boarding area.

The children must ask for permission to pet any cat we are boarding. They are only allowed to touch or pet cats that are friendly and comfortable with children and whose owners we know would not mind. Some customers prefer children not be around their cats and we strictly honor that request. Some cats that are quite friendly get spooked by children, for whatever reason we do not know. They will start hissing the minute they see one of the little folk.

If we have a cat that is aggressive in the inn we never allow the cat and a child to have any chance of contact. We always tell the children never ever to put their face near any cat to avoid any chance of a startled cat scratching them. Fast movements when close to cats is not a good thing as startled cats can do weird things.

Most of the children that have lived in our home want to help with the cats and don't want to be banished so we have had very few infractions of the rules. My grandchildren and foster children have learned how to care responsibly for the animals. They love to collect the dirty food dishes out of the units, dump the water dishes so we can give the cats fresh water, and delivering meals to the kitties, who are of course, very happy to see them coming. This is big stuff for five to ten year olds, and it has helped many of our foster children learn valuable lessons about how to care for and show love to creatures dependent on them – lessons many of them never learned in their birth homes. Although having the children "helping" slows me down quite a bit, seeing many of the underprivileged children we have fostered grow is a reward that is hard to duplicate. It can be a richly rewarding experience. (See story, "The Cat That Healed A Little Girl").

PAYMENT METHODS

We accept checks or cash in payment, but not credit cards. We ask for checks because it makes our record keeping easier. Ninety percent of our customers pay with checks.

Because we are the only luxury B&B facility in our locale, the credit card issue has never been a problem. If a competitor moved in nearby, we might have to change that policy. I know similar operations to ours that operate in major metropolitan areas (think New York city) that take credit cards to avoid bad check risk and for the convenience of their customers. Those operations also require deposits, and that is hard to do without accepting credit cards. We have only had four to five bad checks in the seventeen years we have been in business. If we had been paying credit card fees all those years, I am sure we would be looking at 15 – 20k in additional overhead costs during that time instead of $750.00 in bad checks.

Each of these business policies we outline is an individual matter that has worked well for us, but every business owner must make their own decisions and seek professional counsel where needed.

DEPOSITS

Taking deposits on reservations is closely related to the credit card issue as mentioned. We do not ask for deposits. We only ask people to please call us and let us know if their plans change as it allows us to provide the space to another cat owner who needs to board their kitty. We only average three to four no-shows a year, as most people do call us when they need to cancel. The few no-shows we encounter have not been sufficient to make us feel we need to change this policy. Again, in a major metropolitan area, this policy may not work. When conducting your market survey find out what competitive establishment policies are. If they all require deposits, you can safely assume that they probably have good reason for doing so.

CATS ONLY – NO DOGS ALLOWED

I have some good friends that are dogs – so I am not anti-dog. Many cats also get along quite well with their canine counterparts. When cats are out of their home surroundings, however, unfamiliar barking and growling dogs can be a source of severe stress. This would make their boarding stay an unpleasant experience. Our "cats only" environment has been a key ingredient in our success.

CONTRACTS

When we first started we used contracts for every customer. It was not long before we abandoned using them except for special circumstances. We have always put the customer and their cat first, and for us, that has avoided some of the typical problems encountered in the customer relations area. We are boarding a member of the family for our customers – and we treat all their cats just like we treat our own – with lots of love and care. Cat owners are great people, and they will appreciate it when you put out that kind of effort. Many of our customers board with us multiple times a year, and continued contract signing would be pointless. Having a long-term agreement with these customers on file to cover any issues that arise with their cat is an option. Our contract has done the job for us over the years, and hopefully this will continue. You should make sure to get legal approval, however, of any binding contract you use for your own protection.

In special circumstances, where a cat has a severe health issue, such as heart problem or serious renal disease, the risk always exists he/she might pass away while the owner is absent. In such situations we do execute the contract to make sure we have the required permissions for treatment and that the customer agrees to cover the cost of any vet bills incurred.

If we have a nagging feeling when a cat is being dropped off that the owner might be a risk for abandoning the cat we have them sign a contract. The contract should cover, in specific language, exactly what will happen if an owner does not pick up the cat in a timely manner.

VISITORS

Visitors have a tendency to want to touch the cats in the boarding area. It just seems to come naturally to cat lovers. The cats seem to enjoy visitors also (somewhat the reverse of the zoo psychology —"Oh, look at the interesting humans") and will rub around inviting attention and caressing. It is best if people not go around from cat to cat touching each one because that is a good way to spread germs. We try to discourage the touching as much as possible as there is also the risk a cat could scratch or nip someone. Here again, there can be liability issues with a customer being injured, so check with your legal counsel on how you should handle this matter.

HOURS

Deciding on the schedule of hours to be open is a balancing act between meeting customer needs and having a life. Some customers want to come all hours of the day and night, and we had to decide where to draw the line. Since we operate out of our home we have to endure the, "Well, you're there anyhow, and getting kitty at 8:30 pm Tuesday night will work for me" attitude. Most customers are more thoughtful than this, but there are always those exceptions and we had to learn how to say, "I'm sorry, but we just can't be here at that time on Tuesday. We can do around 5:00 pm- 6:00 pm, or early Wednesday morning if you would prefer." But, situations do arise where we just have to help out, like our customer who has to catch the ferry back to Nantucket to get home and who can't change the ferry schedule to meet kitty's exit time.

We decided when we first opened that we might be better off if we just stressed that we worked by appointment exclusively. Although we do have approximate drop off hours, we aways schedule an appointment. This allows us to meet customer needs but also plan our own lives. Our target times for departures and arrivals is around 10:00 am in the morning and between 4:00 to 5:00 pm in the afternoon. This gives us the mid portion of the day for our own activities. The afternoon hours have also always combined nicely with the time we need to be home to meet the foster children's afternoon school bus. On Saturday we are open from 9:00 am till noon, and on Sunday from 5:00 to 6:00 pm. We have always made some Sunday hours available due to the fact most people returning from vacations have to be at work on Monday morning. People are encouraged to pick up their cats at 10:00 am by not charging for the day if the cat leaves at that time, so this is similar to the way most human hotels operate. We do try to accommodate people who have difficult travel schedules and this does give us a competitive advantage over commercial establishments that have to maintain well defined and not always flexible hours due to staffing constraints. Over the past couple of years we have become more flexible on Sunday appointments to enhance our competitive position.

It is ideal to have all cleaning and feeding activities completed by the time people start arriving. Customers usually want to look around at all the other cats when they arrive, and early morning in the cat room is not the "prettiest" part of the day since cats have a predilection for making a mess during the night. As appreciation of the cats is a major part of the customer experience, we want to look our best when they arrive. If we have to do a 9:00 am appointment, we just try to be all cleaned up at that time. If, for some reason a customer just has to come earlier than 9:00 am, we say, "We can do it, but please appreciate that we aren't at our best at that hour of the morning." Most people understand this and are appreciative that you are going the extra mile to help them out. When you're dealt lemons, make lemonade!

CUSTOMER SUPPLIED ITEMS

• **Food** – We encourage customers to bring some items and discourage them from bringing others. If a customer wants to keep their kitty on the same diet they are on at home and bring their own food we accommodate that request. It does cause some extra work, as we have to keep track of and store food for multiple kitties in the boarding room, but it also provides some benefits. Cats have a tendency to refuse to eat for a day or so when they first arrive, so familiar is often better. Most cats will start eating a bit faster after arriving at the inn if they have familiar food from home.

Some facilities charge extra to feed cats their own food due to the logistic issues – making sure staff feeds the right food to the right cat, etc. Since I have no staff and am the primary caregiver, I can keep track of all the foods and cats in my head. When really busy, I simply label the foods with the cats name. We don't charge for the service because we have found that most customers will leave food (especially the canned food) and that helps to lower our costs and makes the policy a win/win for us and the customer. People who bring dry food often leave it "for all the other kitties" at the inn and that works out fine also.

Another benefit of feeding cats their own food is that a significant number of cats have "quirky" stomachs, and many times their owners have spent a lot of time identifying food that kitty won't "up-chuck." Avoiding the up-chuck issue is easier on kitty and innkeeper, as we won't have to be doing quite so much cleaning up after them. Some cats also get diarrhea when fed wet food. Their system, for some reason, just can't seem to handle wet food. Others have the same problem with dry food.

• **Bedding** – We encourage people to bring their kitty's bed and/or favorite sleeping blanket. This helps make them more at ease in their new environment and it helps tremendously on minimizing laundry and associated costs. It is definitely a win/win situation.

• **Toys** – If people want to bring toys we put them in the unit with the kitties. We do not have "community" toys in the boarding area for all the cats to play with due to the risk of spreading germs.

• **Food Dishes, Litter, And Litter Pans** – We discourage customers from bringing any of these items. I have never found a cat yet that will not use the litter box because of the litter. There have been a few that would not use the litter box all the time because they did not want to use the litter box period - never mind what kind of litter was in it. Cats are basically pretty clean creatures, and they don't want to "mess up their own nest" and have to live in it. Using customer litter is a big storage problem and hinders a speedy cleaning operation.

Customer supplied food dishes also complicates things. They are always getting left behind when customers leave. Dishes are usually dirty from the last meal kitty enjoyed when customers come to pick up their cats, and getting food dishes cleaned for pickup time is one more complication of an already complicated schedule. We avoid customer supplied food dishes as much as possible. From time to time we will get a case that is an exception for a really good reason. One situation I can remember is a cat that would not drink from a bowl. He was particularly fond of drinking from running water (under a faucet). We finally had to wire a rabbit watering bottle that hung on the inside of the screen door with the drinking tube extending below the bottle for kitty to lick from. The cat accepted the bottle, licking from the tube and evidently seemed convinced it was an acceptable substitute for a running faucet. The customer was right – that was the only way that darn cat would drink. We do have a couple of customers who just insist that their kitty has to have pine litter, or a stainless steel litter pan, but most people are reasonable about using our standard litter box.

We use Corningware™ food dishes. They are tough, store neatly, and fit in the dishwasher easily. We always use glass or ceramic food dishes. Some cats are allergic to plastic and aluminum and can develop acne on their chin from rubbing against the bowl.

• **Medicines** – People with cats on medications are an important target market segment. Getting medications into kitty is important to these customers, and boarding is the absolute best way to make sure the kitty gets its meds.

Many people will have a friend or family member come by their house to feed and check up on kitty, but some cats will make themselves "unavailable" as soon as someone they are uncomfortable with tries to shove some pills down their throat. The problem is that once they decide this pill operation "ain't gonna fly," they know every possible place to hide in the house. In the boarding situation, the cat is in a defined area and cannot escape their duly appointed "pill giver." Thus kitty gets meds as required.

We regularly board cats on medications for thyroid, asthma, heart, and urinary issues. Diabetic cats require regular insulin shots. We've even had a few cats requiring hydration therapy. Hydration therapy involves insertion of a syringe under the skin and allowing a specified amount of saline solution to flow from an IV bag to help hydrate the cat. An innkeeper will definitely want to get professional advice when considering performing this service

Many medications can be placed in the cats wet food. Pills can be ground up and mixed into the wet food, and many cats will eat the wet food including the pill without grinding it up. Pill treats also help to get pills into cats. I frequently put a pill inside a pill pocket and then press a couple of those Temptation™ "treats" into the soft sides of the pill pocket. Most cats are so enamored of the treats that they gobble down the whole assembly in a flash.

Diabetic cats require insulin shots, and the procedure is pretty simple once you get the hang of it. It does help to have a second person hold the cat while the other administers the shot. My wife and I give the shots together and that has worked fine for us. It is much easier to safely give the shot if the cat is held securely when you insert the needle. Local vets or vet techs will often teach inn-keepers how to do it. It's pretty simple once you get comfortable with the idea and master the technique.

We have recently found a great way to get pills into obstinate cats. Drop the pill (break or crush if necessary) into a syringe (not hypodermic, but oral type) with a bit of water in it and let pill dissolve. We do this by removing the plunger from the body of the syringe, putting a bit of water in it, then dropping the pill in. We reinsert the plunger, let the pill fully dissolve, then squirt the fluid with med into the back of the cat's throat.

CHAPTER 12

CAT HEALTH/MEDICAL

Familiarity with cat health and ailments afflicting felines is important. I am not a veterinarian, vet tech or feline medical expert. I do not pretend to be an expert in such subjects, but have learned as much as I can so as to be knowledgeable about areas of cat health that will affect my business. I want to protect my customers' beloved kitties and that requires possessing sufficient knowledge to enable me take proper precautions to prevent the spread of any illnesses we encounter. Although there is no way to be sure of preventing the spread of illness (even after all precautions have been taken) the likelihood of such an event can be minimized by properly arming oneself with knowledge.

It is a good idea to establish a relationship with at least one vet that can be called if and when there is a question or problem. Most vets are willing to be helpful, and the fact that you will be boarding many of their clients gives them somewhat of a vested interest in assisting you in protecting your guests. Whenever possible, call the vet for the cat involved in the issue you are facing. Vets appreciate your respecting their relationship with their customer.

The following discussion of medical issues is limited to areas that are particularly relevant to operating a boarding facility.

VACCINES

FVRCP and Rabies are the two most important vaccines from a boarding facility's perspective. The first vaccination we will discuss is the FVRCP. FVRCP is a combination vaccine and the letters stand for Feline Viral Rhinotracheitis, Calcivirus, and Panleukopenia, and the vaccination helps provide protection against these three maladies.

Feline Viral Rhinotracheitis is an upper respiratory infection (URI) somewhat similar to human influenza. (Please note the difference between UTI and URI, as sometimes the names sound similar in conversation, and UTI stands for Urinary Tract Infection.) A URI is caused by the feline herpesvirus-1, so you will sometimes hear the disease referred to as a herpes infection. The symptoms can include watery runny eyes, swollen or ulcerated eyes, sneezing, nasal congestion, oral ulcerations, coughing and frequently general malaise and lack of appetite. URI infections are highly contagious and can be spread by airborne particles resulting from sneezing, by direct contact with the infected animal, or even by contact with caretakers who have been touching or around the sick cat. A cat with a URI should be isolated as soon as the problem is identified and caretakers should use extreme care in hand washing and make sure not to use any items or tools involved with the infected cat on any healthy animals. Separate water containers, food supplies, litter scoops etc. are best used for the infected animal.

Calcivirus is a virus that afflicts the respiratory system and all of the techniques discussed above should be observed.

A common danger with upper respiratory ailments is the risk of secondary infections. Although many URIs run their course and the cat recovers, in severe cases the cats will develop a secondary infection which can end up in pneumonia. Seek assistance from your vet when the cat does not seem to be getting over the original URI. You don't want the kitty to get really ill.

Panleukopenia is the third disease covered by the FVRCP shot. This ailment is also referred to as Feline Distemper. Panleukopenia causes an ulcerated intestinal lining, diarrhea, intestinal bleeding and dehydration that leads to further susceptibility to bacterial infections. This disease has a very high mortality rate.

Rabies has a 100% mortality rate in cats. It is nearly 100% fatal in humans also if proper treatment is not received immediately after being bitten by an infected animal. This is the reason most states require all cats be vaccinated against rabies.

There are two types of rabies vaccines – adjuvanted (killed) and non-adjuvanted. The "old" three year rabies shots are adjuvanted (they use a killed vaccine) and the one year non-adjuvanted shot uses modified live viruses. Adjuvanted vaccines have been associated with injection site sarcomas and for that reason some vets avoid giving the three year shot. The reason is not that the vets are trying to drum up more business by giving yearly shots, although the non-adjuvanted vaccines have been less costly for vets to purchase. Non-adjuvanted vaccinations have been safer although they did have to be repeated on a yearly basis. Purevax has recently introduced a three year non-adjuvanted vaccine that seems to be quickly becoming the preferred standard for the rabies vaccination.

One additional bit of information. Studies have shown the yearly rabies shot provides protection for more than one year, but the clinical approval trials had some minor discrepancies that resulted in the vaccine not being legally approved to claim multi-year protection. For more information on this subject and the whole area of feline vaccinations spend some time on **www.catinfo.org**. Be sure to obtain professional counsel on how to handle this area.

Please note that the law requires vaccination of all cats. "Inside" cats are not excluded under the law because they do not go "outside." Bats, for example, are the most frequently occurring transmission source of rabies to human beings due to their ability to infiltrate a house through windows, chimneys, the attic, etc. An inside cat can be exposed just as easily as we can. We also have to face the possibility the cat could get outside in some emergency situation – think flooding, fire, hurricane, tornado and more.

I have boarded inside cats that were not up to date on their rabies vaccination for one reason or another, but I am extremely cautious in such situations. I am not suggesting that you accept cats that have not had the rabies shot. You can't be too careful where rabies is concerned. If you have a questionable situation arise, seek professional medical counsel.

Feline Leukemia does not seem to be considered highly contagious by most of the sources I have referred to. The virus does not live very long outside the body of the infected animal, so it is not quite as contagious as I once thought. The FeLV shots have been the source of frequent injection site tumors, and for this reason many vets do not recommend FeLV vaccination unless there is a very good reason. A healthy cat living with an HIV infected cat, for example, might be a situation where the shot would be given to the healthy cat due to its close and extended contact with the HIV positive animal. I have boarded five or six three legged cats that had to endure leg amputations due to injection site carcinomas.

From a boarding point of view, I have had a few HIV positive guests, and I always isolate them from the other cats and use separate tools and supplies in caring for them to avoid any possibility of cross contamination. We have never had a problem with transmission of the disease to another boarder.

ADDITIONAL HEALTH CONSIDERATIONS

Sneezing – Since sneezing is associated with upper respiratory ailments, a sneezing cat is cause for immediate concern. But sneezing can result from other conditions also, so it is a judgment call. With experience it becomes easier to decide what course of action to take, but if the cat shows any other signs of getting sick (watery/runny eyes, runny nose, coughing, constantly licking its lips) isolate the cat right away. Whenever a cat sneezes, if in doubt, it is better to isolate the cat than to take a chance on a URI epidemic in the boarding area.

We do find that some cats that sneeze are not getting sick. One little persian kitty called Rusty boarded with us for 13 years, and he would always get excited and sneeze when I served his newly replenished food dish. I have seen this happen with a number of cats. Others have sneezed when the windows are opened and the fresh air starts flowing through the room. This probably is a result of allergies. I have noticed a high percentage of the otherwise healthy sneezers were of persian, himalayan and siamese heritage.

One additional point to keep in mind. A cat that has had a URI in the past can shed the virus for years – sort of a bit like a "typhoid Mary" syndrome – even though the cat shows absolutely no sign of being sick. This makes the whole sneezing issue a tough one to deal with for the innkeeper. If I know a cat has had a URI in the past and it starts sneezing, I isolate it from the other cats right away. The cat could be shedding the virus when sneezing even if it is only allergies that are prompting the sneezing.

The cat to worry about is the one who sneezes for no apparent reason and just looks like it may not be feeling good. Add watery or runny eyes, runny nose and we get isolate them pronto. URIs are very contagious and the bane of feline innkeepers. After years of experience, I get a gut feeling from just looking at the cat that it may have a problem. It is like looking at your child and knowing he/she is coming down with something.

Runny eye by itself may or may not be a problem. You will run into cats that have a runny eye but appear otherwise healthy. This is often a leftover sign of a previous herpes infection. You may want to ask the cat's vet if that is the case and if the cat is currently healthy and ok to board. Interestingly, many vets proscribe a daily dose of L-Lysine as a way of strengthening the cats immune system against the virus. After being sick with bronchitis and pneumonia for four years, I started taking a 500 mg L-lysine tablet morning and night and have not even had a cold since.

Coughing can be related to a URI infection, but there are other reasons a cat may cough. A retching cough is rather common amongst cats suffering from a hairball. If the cough persists for more than a day or two we consult their vet. We have had cats cough up round worms, a rather unpalatable situation requiring a worming medication regimen. Fleas can also be a source of infection with worms, a result of the cats ingesting fleas while they are grooming themselves.

This section is only intended as a quick introduction to the subject and to convey the importance of making sure the animals hosted in a kitty B&B have been properly vaccinated. It is the key step in keeping the cats safe. There is no assurance that following these procedures will prevent incidents of sickness from occurring, but at least everything possible will have been done to protect guests.

We encourage everybody to learn all they can about cat health. It will be a great asset in operating a successful kitty hotel business. There is a tremendous amount of good information on the Internet provided by veterinarians and universities, and Cornell University's site for veterinary medicine is terrific.

CHAPTER 13

TIPS AND STRATEGIES

This chapter describes ideas and tips that have made our life in the cat house easier. Many of these ideas improve the boarding experience for the cat, cat owner and innkeeper.

INTRODUCING THE CAT TO ITS ROOM AT THE INN

1. Accommodations - Have the cat's room all set up and add his/her bed (blanket, shirt or whatever the owner brings from home) on arrival. Add cat's toys and they are set to go in their condo.

2. Food - Make sure cat has plenty of fresh water and a supply of dry food if applicable. Cats that have dry food at home usually have it available in the unit 24-7. Wet food is served two times a day.

3. Individual Care - One reason people board pets is that they're on some kind of medication. Some cats get insulin shots twice daily, others get thyroid medicine once or twice daily and so on. All cats should be checked on to make sure they are eating, drinking and using their potty box.

Always ask customers if they would like to bring the food the cat eats at home. Keeping them on the their home diet helps with cats that have digestive issues when fed certain types of food, something the B&B owner would not be aware of. Owner supplied food cuts down on costs, but can increase complexity of feeding if you have staff to deal with.

Most cats, especially those that have previously boarded, will be fairly calm when they arrive. Even so, we always leave the cat in their and put the carrier in the condo because it is easier on the cat and safer for me, in the event the cat panics for some reason. A few arrivals will be upset and they can get aggressive. For this reason, any upset (grumbling, growling, hissing) cat is always put in the condo in their carrier – no exceptions. Once the unit is set up with bed, water and food in place, we carefully open the door to their carrier and shut the condo door. Most cats will stay in the back of the carrier while the carrier door is opened and many will remain in their carrier for quite a while till they get accustomed to their new environment. Some, however, will leap at the door of the carrier as it is opened, clawing and attempting to get a piece of me. If the cat is visibly upset, we are very careful as we attempt to un-latch the carrier door because some cats can get their razor sharp claws through the carrier door and into our hands.

Placing the carrier with the cat still residing in it inside the condo allows the cat to remain, where for the moment, it is relatively comfortable. Many cats will remain in the carrier for quite awhile, but rest assured, they will come out when they get acclimated. A few cats are content sleeping in their carrier, so just leave the carrier in the unit for them. Many times I leave the carrier in the cat's unit for the duration of their stay. Sometimes I remove the door from the carrier so it is not getting in their way.

When designing and building your condos, make sure you have sufficient room between the floor of the unit and the first shelf to be able to slide even large carriers in place. Usually this is not a problem, as you will also most likely have a covered potty box on the floor of the unit which will usually be fairly high. We built our large condos units with 23" inches of clearance from the floor to the bottom of the first shelf. The studio units have 19" clearance.

SAFETY GLOVES

I have a pair of Kevlar gloves with arm protectors that go up to my elbows. I always have these gloves in the boarding room. In a pinch, the really heavy insulated fireplace/woodstove gloves will work, but I did get myself bitten while wearing stove gloves, heavy as they are. In that case, the cat's bite just happened to land right in the sewn seam along the side of the finger. The canine teeth penetrated through the seam and went right into my finger. I have not relied on those types of gloves since. The Kevlar gloves cost one hundred dollars or more, but they are worth every penny when face to face with a cat that has declared war and obviously has a black belt in feline karate.

The arm protectors are also important. A few cats seem to regard the process of being stuffed into a carrier as an imminent threat to their existence. Sharp clawed paws flailing franticly in all directions can tear up hands and arms in a flash. With upset cats we wear the gloves.

When a really upset cat arrives at the inn, everybody will know. The minute a hand gets near the door of the carrier there will be an eruption and obvious attempt to do damage. With these little charmers we have to wear the Kevlar gloves to undo the carrier door latches. It's a bit clumsy, but it beats getting those claws sunk into my hand. Usually, however, this same cat becomes my best buddy after I feed him for a couple of days.

PEOPLE BRINGING CATS WITHOUT A CARRIER

A few people come to the door holding their cat in their arms. This is very dangerous, as all it takes is a car backfire, motorcycle racing down the street or firecracker thrown from a car and the kitty may just bolt from their owner's arms.

One customer not using a carrier had his cat panic when it arrived at the door and smelled the other cats. The kitty bolted, scratching him up pretty good while escaping and headed for nearby woods. So we then had a customer bleeding all over the place and a kitty to try to coax out of the woods. We set up a lawn chair for our customer, got him a newspaper and coffee, and he spent the morning calling dear "Scruffy" from the wood's edge. He finally had to leave to get some lunch, then returned to spend the afternoon crooning out soothing tunes to Scruffy, who was having none of it. Realizing the hour was approaching that good old Scruffy usually got pretty hungry, he placed a bowl of dry food near his chair and Scruffy finally succumbed. It was a very long day!

We encourage people to use a carrier. Some however, will not do it for one reason or another, and I guess we just have to live with that and just get them in the door quickly when they arrive to minimize the chance of the cat escaping.

SENIOR CATS AND KITTENS

Our studio units were designed and built with senior cats and kittens in mind. The shelf in these units are closer to the floor than in our large units. For seniors that have trouble jumping, this makes life a lot easier. We can also put stools in the units so cats can walk to the upper shelf. Young kittens get to reside in these units also since they get totally absorbed with their frolicking, and we worry that in a large unit they could fall and hurt themselves. There is no danger of this happening in the smaller unit.

ARTISTIC CATS

You laugh? How could a cat possibly be artistic enough to paint? Easy. First you play in your water bowl. Then, once your paws are really soaked, you climb into the litter box full of clay litter and walk around for a while. Once the feet are properly prepared, you exit the potty box and parade around the condo pausing briefly now and then to admire the distinctive pattern feline foot pads make on the floor. Now, back to the water bowl for one more pass, a quick trip through the litter pan and you are ready to paint your wall mural. Sitting or standing in front of the wall, you carefully slide your paws up and down repeatedly, depositing long litter-gray colored brush strokes up, down and across the wall. Cleaning up after Van Gogh every morning gets old real fast – like the second time it happens.

For these talented felines, I immediately switch to a wood pellet or crystal type litter, so there is nothing to smear all over the place. I always make sure to have a bag of feline grade wood pellet litter around (as well as some of the crystal type). Fuel wood pellets cannot be used as those products frequently contain chemicals that can be harmful to the cats. When the cat grooms itself, it can ingest particles of the litter contaminated with chemicals.

The feline wood pellet litter is less expensive than the crystal product, but you will be glad to have either on hand when you find yourself hosting an "artistic" cat.

ACTIVITIES

In case you have never noticed, cats are pretty good at entertaining themselves. Cats also exercise isometrically as you have probably seen them do. Some cats will come out of their condo and spend time "introducing themselves" to the other cats, sometimes with hilarious results - other times they will get quite friendly with their neighbor. We have even had some "romances" develop. Many cats are quite happy sleeping in their condos and either will not come out, or will come out walk around a bit then go right back to their condo to take another nap.

We only allow cats out by family (if there are two or more boarding together from the same family) or one at a time for individual guests. We never let cats from separate families out together. There is always the risk of a fracas, or the increased potential for spreading one type or another of feline germs. I know there are many places that do this, but we will never do it. The risks outweigh any possible benefit, and most customers do not like the idea.

PAPER FOOD TRAYS

We decided early on that the best way to serve food was to use paper trays for wet food. We use glass and ceramic dishes (finally deciding on Corningware) for water bowls and dry food. Wet food is messy and using regular dinnerware would result in running the dishwasher excessively. Paper trays are used for one wet meal and thrown. This gives kitty a nice clean plate for its wet food twice a day. The dishes for dry food and water can be used multiple days and then run through the dishwasher when the cat leaves.

Paper food trays (one-half pound size works well) can be found at most restaurant supply stores or on Amazon. Avoid plastic and aluminum dishes as some cats are allergic to those materials.

VACUUM

We opted for an industrial grade vacuum for cleaning in our business. We are cleaning units every day at least once, and having a vacuum with a wand cleaning attachment avoids a lot of on-your-hands-and-knees cleaning. We selected an Orek industrial grade cannister model and it has performed exceedingly well for us. Cats can make quite a mess overnight, and this vacuum quickly and effortlessly gobbles up most of the mess.

We have equipped the machine with a 20' crushproof hose so we can reach every unit in our boarding area. The "crushproof" feature is important as the hose will get stepped on frequently and suffer various other sorts of abuse during its lifetime. We have never regretted spending the money for the good crushproof hose. We had to attach this special order hose to the factory issue hose connector that connects to the cannister, but the hose pretty much just screws in. The Oreck store can also set it up. The industrial vac is a bit noisy, but most cats quickly adjust then ignore it. Some will play with the nozzle end while I vacuum which is a funny sight.

I have found the vac has also worked for me as a defensive tool when working with aggressive cats. For some reason, most aggressive cats have more respect for the business end of the vac than do more peaceable kitties. In our large units, almost all of the aggressive cats will head for the top shelf of the unit when confronted with the business end of the vac while I am cleaning. When dealing with an aggressive cat, it is important to stay below the level of the cat. If you are face to face with the cat and level with him, he may attack, especially if you have eye contact. I stay below the cat and avoid eye contact. This seems to impart a message of submission to the cat. Coming at them on the level with eye contact conveys a message of aggression.

If the cat is still faking lunges at me, I hold the business end (the head is on the end of the 4 four foot Orek wand) of the hissing vac above my head and between the cat and myself while I clean the unit. That has almost always worked for me.

So the vac continues to serve two critical functions in our B&B, and it has been functioning perfectly in this role for 17 years. We installed the cannister itself below our "Tower Condo," which just so happens to have a perfectly sized space for the unit. This location also helps muffle the noise of the vac motor.

If I was building our facility from scratch again, I would install a built-in vacuum system and locate the vacuum motor/cannister where it would be hidden from view.

CHAPTER 14

THE CAT THAT HEALED A LITTLE GIRL

The little girl emerging from the car was tall for her seven years, bedraggled and rail thin. Straight, sandy brown hair hung down over her shoulders, framing a pale but pretty face with big green eyes. Her jeans were tight at the waist and three inches short of her bony ankles, where tattered canvas sneakers, one with flopping sole, showed the best she had to wear was last summer's clothes. Her mother had not been able to care for her, the father refused, and so she remained in the foster care system. This would be her sixth foster home in less than a year and she looked exhausted.

There was a glint of defiance in her eyes, a symptom of the smoldering resentment buried deep in her heart. The anger resulted in volatile behavior that could erupt at the slightest provocation. None of the five previous homes had been able to cope with the behaviors arising from her tortured past, and thus her painful journey continued.

Shaylin had lived in a situation of gross parental neglect forcing her to care for her two-year-old brother when she was less than five herself. She changed diapers, prepared food and dressed her brother when her mother could not. It all ended one frigid evening when police found the two children, clad only in their pajamas, on the street. Thus one formidable struggle ended and another began.

Those painful early years left Shaylin in a state psychiatrists call "parentified." Parentification is partially a result of children attempting to assume responsibilities far beyond their years. The struggle to obtain basic human needs against overwhelming odds generates a powerful impulse in a child to attempt to control their environment to avoid the pain caused by neglect. Parentified children also have great difficulty accepting the authority and decisions of adults around them and usually end up butting heads with everyone in a never-ending struggle for control.

These factors had combined to produce a little girl social services could not keep in a home for any meaningful length of time. She was, at the time of her first respite visit with us, on the ropes once again.

Her foster mother at the time was desperately in need of a break and would shortly give up on her too, although we had no knowledge of that at the time. On her second respite stay we were told her next stop would be an institution.

There was some indefinable quality about Shaylin that tugged at our heart. The grim prospect of seeing her thrown into the uproar typical of an institution full of deeply disturbed children plunged us into dismay. Except for the irresponsibility of the adults in her life, she would not be in this predicament. Surely, we thought, someone would help her. But social services had finally given up. We could not bear seeing Shaylin institutionalized and pleaded with the agency to give us the opportunity to work with her. Although skeptical, they finally agreed.

The state of affairs at the foster home Shaylin was living had degraded to the point they wanted her out immediately. They would not even keep her for two more weeks until we returned from a long planned vacation. She had to be respited at an emergency placement home in the interim.

The day after our return from vacation Shaylin arrived. All the possessions she had in the world were packed in three plastic trash bags that barely outweighed her own 48 pounds. Unfortunately, she had far more emotional baggage than physical possessions.

In one of the previous foster homes Shaylin had been accused of kicking a toy poodle and breaking its rib. The catalyst for this event was evidently Shaylin's perception that the owner of the dog had been mean to her. The incident also included additional charges she attempted to poison the dog by sprinkling laundry flakes into the dog's food. We never found out if the charges were true, but needless to say, the report caused us concern as to the safety of our own four cats. Thus Shaylin was forbidden to touch or even be near the cats.

Rajah, our tiger kitty, had been our grandaughter's cat until she developed allergies, and then he came to live with us. Although aloof much of the time, Rajah missed the children he grew up with. He had evidently decided Shaylin had been with us long enough and seemed puzzled by her refusal to respond to his offers of friendship. From time to time he would walk by her and rub against her leg, a maneuver resulting in a most uncomfortable look on Shaylin's face, as she did not know quite what to do.

We began to realize, in light of Rajah's steadily increasing attentions, we would have to modify the rules in some manner. Since careful observation had revealed no signs of ill intent towards the cats on Shaylin's part, we decided to allow her to have contact with Rajah in the living room as long as we were present.

Rajah capitalized on this opportunity. He would stride across the living room, jump up on Shaylin's lap, and contentedly sit as she stroked his back for what seemed an interminable length of time for a seven year old diagnosed with attention deficit disorder. Most amazing, all the attention she lavished on Rajah was done in a caring, gentle manner, a trait Shaylin was not exactly known for.

For some reason Rajah had taken a real shine to Shaylin, and he started exhibiting behavior we had not observed before. He would regularly appear in the yard about the time Shaylin's school bus arrived each day. As Shaylin ran from the bus to the house, Rajah would trot alongside, bolting in front of her at the last minute to make sure he did not get left outside. Later, as Shaylin sat on the living room couch doing her homework, Rajah would be comfortably curled up at her side.

At Shaylin's bedtime a very regular pattern of activities was always followed. Repetition is helpful in keeping parentified children on track. Knowing the schedule and her responsibilities helped Shaylin deal with the ever-present temptation to start making up rules of her own.

On being told it was time for bed Shaylin would head off to the downstairs bathroom to brush her teeth. Then it was time to give us both a goodnight hug and head off to bed. It did not take Rajah long to figure out the routine. After we had been given our hug, he would either be waiting by the hallway door or trotting alongside Shaylin as she left the living room and headed up to bed.

We had had numerous behavior issues with Shaylin during this period, but gratefully none were related to the cats. One major concern was a result of the horrible nightmares Shaylin suffered. Buried memories of past trauma escape the deepest corridors of the mind at night, and the nightmares produced make it impossible to achieve restful sleep. In the beginning we were often awakened by Shaylin's screams – screams so electrifying we were jarred out of a sound sleep and propelled down the hallway to make sure she was ok. We would arrive at her door only to find she had locked or barred the door, her method of keeping out intruders like those she had encountered in the past. As a result we had to insist Shaylin leave her bedroom door cracked open at night so we could check on her and see she was safe, but maintaining that unlocked door policy was a battle that continued for months. We finally told her if she wanted Rajah to sleep with her she had to leave the door ajar so he could get out to use his potty box at night. From that time on the door was never again a problem. Shaylin placed a very high value on having her beloved friend with her where, nestled together, they were secure sharing their mutual and unconditional love.

Shaylin had been with us a several months when we went in one night to check on her. She was sleeping peacefully, an angelic look on her face, a picture we usually only had the pleasure of observing when she was sound asleep. Her head was on the pillow facing away from us and her arm was wrapped around a bulge in the blanket drawn up against her chest. Carefully parting the folds in order to pull the blanket over her, we uncovered a very relaxed Rajah, who upon being disturbed from his rest sleepily raised his eyes to meet mine, as if asking for what reason I was intruding into his cozy lair.

Rajah was a good friend, and his love was becoming an increasingly important factor in Shaylin's healing. Once he started sleeping with her the frequency of the nightmares declined steadily.

Rajah, it seemed, had the key to penetrating Shaylin's troubled exterior, applying just the right amount of healing balm to her agitated soul. Many times, after getting herself in trouble, something she was prone to do on a rather regular basis, Shaylin would be sent to her room, where she could be heard vociferously complaining to Rajah, as if he were capable of understanding, in the minutest detail, just how unfair we were.

Never once in her stay in our home did Shaylin hurt Rajah and the bond between the two grew ever deeper. The only time she ever gave us pause was when she trimmed some fur from Rajah's back with a pair of scissors. The cutting was so slight it was almost indistinguishable, and I probably would never have noticed had Carol not pointed it out to me. Troubled children often find the act of cutting with scissors a calming influence. Frequently, Shaylin would cut a number of full-sized sheets of paper into a pile of strips. During one of these cutting sessions she had evidently been tempted to give Rajah a gentle trim. Although we were upset, we also realized an overreaction on our part could be a disaster to Shaylin's progress. A punishment forbidding contact with Rajah, for example, could set her back months. We finally decided the best course would be to sit down and talk with Shaylin and rely on her love for Rajah to carry us through. Carol and I talked at length, emphasizing the responsibility we have to care for our little friends and stressing how much Rajah loved and trusted her. Shaylin sat and stroked Rajah all the time we were talking, and from the look on her face, we could tell she was truly sorry that she might have violated Rajah's trust.

That first year with Shaylin was a tumultuous time, one that in and of itself could fill a book. We would take two steps forward, one backward and start over again. But ever so slowly progress was being achieved. Carol's combination of motherly care mixed with firm discipline and predictable repetition was a vital part of the picture, as was Rajah's love. Shaylin also found something else she never had before. In me, she seemed to have found the father figure she so desperately wanted. Many evenings Shaylin would come into my office to say goodnight, climb up in my lap and tell me about her day and the problems she had. In an attempt to help her I would sometimes ask about the deeper issues she was wrestling with. The minute our conversation passed some line in the sand that existed in her mind she would look up at me in a sympathetic manner, as if patiently enduring someone who is attempting to be helpful, but is woefully inadequate to the task, and say,

"No, I don't want to talk about that. That's why I have a therapist, Joe."

Her poor therapist, however, couldn't get her to talk with her about many of these issues either, so in at least one limited area of her life she did manage to remain in complete control.

Eventually, when Shaylin was ready to go to bed, she would look into my eyes and whisper "I love you Joe," then scamper out the office door up the stairs and down the hallway to her bedroom where she would join Rajah, who had usually already tucked himself away in her bed. Yes, this little girl who was desperately seeking someone to love and who would love her in return was steadily working her way into the hearts of more than just Rajah.

By the time Shaylin had been with us a year and a half, almost miraculous progress had been achieved, and Social Services decided she was ready for adoption. This was a hard time, for Shaylin had become much more than a "foster child" to us. We had fought her head on, achieved control and made her become a child – a child that could enjoy the security of having responsible adults worry about caring for her. We had, though, through the effort required to modify her behaviors, became emotionally involved.

Emotional involvement, the social agency professionals will tell you, is something that must be avoided. You have to stay "professional," be clinical, remain solely on a therapeutic level. It certainly would have been far easier for us emotionally, as I would learn, if we had maintained distance and stayed on the clinical level, but that is something we found impossible to do.

When Shaylin said, "I love you", she was embarking on a treacherous journey, for she was making herself vulnerable to the rejection she had experienced all her life. It took immense courage for this little girl to take that step, and I found it impossible not to reach back and tell her "I love you too, sweetheart". As I would find, however, when the time came for Shaylin to move on, it would be a painful loss. But, nothing of true value is achieved in life without pain, is it?

Since Carol and I were in our 60's at the time, we realized that we could never be the young parents that a child like Shaylin deserved to have. Parents that could do all the things with her that we had done with our own children. We would be in our 70's before Shaylin would graduate from high school. The mind said one thing and the heart another; but we knew what would be best for Shaylin in the long run would be to find her "forever family."

Shaylin's adoption worker visited to break the news to her. The search for her "forever family" was underway. After the worker left, I walked back into the living room where Shaylin was sitting with Rajah in her lap. Slowly, gently, she stroked his back over and over again as she pensively stared off into space. Once again her future was clouded with uncertainty. What would these developments mean to her and her closest friend in the world?

Eventually the call came and the agency asked if we could meet with a couple interested in adopting Shaylin. Walking into the meeting room, I recognized most of the faces around the table except for a Vietnamese man and Caucasian woman sitting next to him. The social worker rose and introduced us to Hao Pham and his wife Thelma.

The meeting ran quite long as we tried to impart to the Pham's how Shaylin's issues and difficulties would impact them in the future. They seemed undaunted by the potential pitfalls, however, and expressed a desire to proceed.

As we left the meeting and walked out to the parking lot our discussion with the Phams continued. Thelma told us how they had viewed book after book of pictures of children up for adoption but never saw the right child. When the page holding Shaylin's picture was revealed Hao had immediately said,

"That's my little girl."

He would never look back.

A schedule of visits was set up to gradually introduce Shaylin to what we all hoped would be her "forever family." On Hao and Thelma's first visit, we sat in the living room to visit for a while and, hopefully, put Shaylin at ease. Shaylin plopped down in the rocking chair directly across the room from Hao and Thelma and, like a mute, sat and stared at them; it was as if they had just arrived from another planet.

Repeated attempts to engage her in conversation floundered; she just sat and stared.

I could identify with the confused feelings raging in Shaylin's heart, for the same feelings were assailing me too. I felt huge guilt for putting the little girl that said, "I love you Joe," in this position. I was about to leave the room to gather my thoughts and decide what to do when Hao made one last desperate move to save the day. Observing a game of Uno sitting on the bookcase he said,

"Will you play a game of Uno with me?"

Shaylin happened to love to play Uno and Hao's offer presented her with a way to escape the uncomfortable situation, so she somewhat reluctantly accepted his invitation.

We were under instructions to keep the duration of this first visit to no more than a couple of hours. Hao and Thelma had arrived around four o'clock, and the game of Uno started sometime around five. Due to the extreme initial discomfort exhibited by Shaylin, we were all hesitant to call an end to the game playing activity, especially as we began to overhear her softly laughing at Hao's jokes. From time to time cries of "Uno" drifted from the dining room where they were playing. Progress, thankfully, was beginning to occur.

We decided to make some pizza and call a halt to the Uno tournament for supper, but the minute Hao and Shaylin finished their pizza she dragged him right back to the Uno board. Seven o'clock came and went, then eight o'clock, when we finally had to go in and say,

"Shaylin, it's getting late; time to put the game away. Hao and Thelma have a long ride home and it's way past your bedtime."

Thus ended the first visit with Shaylin's "forever family." It began a disaster and ended up a roaring success. After Hao and Thelma left and Shaylin had readied herself for bed she came to give us our regular goodnight hug. As she paused momentarily in front of us, we could see what appeared to be a huge look of relief on her tired little face. With a big sigh, she said,

"I guess I'll sleep good tonight."

As Shaylin and Rajah headed up to bed we were grateful things had turned out far better than we could ever have hoped. It seemed Shaylin might have found her "forever family."

Shaylin began to visit Hao and Thelma for overnight and weekend stays and the legal end of the adoption process was progressing smoothly. Rajah, however, who was used to sleeping with Shaylin every night, found the absences of his little friend confusing.

He would sit in the hallway at the top of the stairs on the nights she was away, eyes fastened on her door, obviously wondering why she was not letting him into the room. But each Sunday night when Shaylin returned, Rajah would welcome her by following her around and being johnny-on-the-spot to climb the stairs and head off to bed.

During our visits with Hao and Thelma we learned about his family's unbelievable story. At the end of the Vietnam War the Pham family had been living in Saigon. Hao's father was imprisoned for "re-education," and Hao was about to be inducted into the army. The Phams were well aware that none of the young men in the neighborhood that had gone into the army in recent years had come back, and Hao's mother had paid off officials to keep Hao's brothers out of the army. By the time Hao's turn came she did not have sufficient funds to meet the officials' demands. The only solution was to get her family out of Vietnam. The heartbreaking decision to leave her husband behind and embark on what turned out to be an epic journey is a story deserving of a book in itself. This courageous little lady spent every last penny she had to purchase a boat on which she and 15 family members and friends would attempt to sail 800 miles from Saigon to the coast of Malaysia and freedom. The escape from Saigon, the harrowing journey by sea complete with a raid by pirates, surviving a perfect storm in The South China Sea, and their eventual arrival in Indonesia where they embarked on the road to freedom and the United States is an awe inspiring tale of human courage. I have often wondered if when Hao first saw Shaylin's photograph, in some mystical way, he sensed that they were kindred spirits, each having survived a harrowing journey against almost insurmountable odds.

The weekend visits had been successful and the official move to her "forever family" was now at the door. With heavy hearts we planned a big party for the day Shaylin would leave. She had become a part of our family and we all needed the opportunity to give her a big and heartfelt farewell.

The big day finally arrived, and our family gathered at our home with Hao and Thelma so we could bid a final farewell to our little girl. Shaylin sat in the same rocking chair she had the first day Hao and Thelma visited and the same look returned to her face. She wanted her "forever family," but she was also about to leave the only peace and security she had ever known in her nine years. As I looked at that little face, guilt was heavy on my heart.

We had to tell Shaylin to open her gifts because she just sat there and stared at them. After finally opening some presents Shaylin returned to the rocker where Sarah, Haley and Leah, three of my granddaughters, gathered around her. Suddenly Sarah started to sniffle. You could see the other two girls fighting back the tears, and then they started jabbering at Sarah, "Don't cry or we're all going to be bawling." I was having trouble fighting back tears myself. Shaylin sat stone still with a stunned look on her face.

It hurt so much to look into the eyes of the little girl who told me, "I love you Joe," and say goodbye.

I was too preoccupied with my own depressed state to be fully aware of the hurt of others for days, but life started to move on and it seemed Carol and I were regaining our balance after Shaylin's departure. But, there was one of us who was not.

Night after night as I went to bed, there, sitting in the upstairs hallway like a statue and expectantly staring down towards Shaylin's door sat Rajah. Time and time again that door had opened and the little girl he loved had come out, gathered him into her arms, and carried him into a land where love without conditions could always be enjoyed.

As I sat down and stroked Rajah's back, he looked down the hall at that door, then up at me, as if only I would open the door his problem would be solved. Tears of sadness ran down my face as my own feelings of loss were intensified by the devotion of this little cat, who I knew would never again experience the comfort of that little girl cradling him in her arms.

For many weeks after Shaylin left I would find Rajah sitting in that hallway looking down the hall towards her door. His faithful watch was an enduring testament to the love that he shared with the little girl that he would never know how much he had helped to heal.

Rajah has gone on to help other young children that have lived with us, but Shaylin was first, and there both we and Rajah will forever hold her in our hearts.

CHAPTER 15

THE ART OF PILLING CATS (AND SHOTS TOO!)

The old medical saw goes, "Take two pills and call me in the morning." Many times this is easier said than done with cats. Pilling some cats can be an exercise in futility, but if you are going to be an innkeeper, you're going to have to find a way to get it done. Some of these innocent looking little creatures can spit out pills almost as fast as a machine gun spews bullets – or maybe it just seems that way. A few we have boarded will "cheek" a pill and wait for you to turn your back before ejecting it. These are the situations where you find the pill lying on the shelf when you are cleaning the unit. It is embarrassing to get outwitted by these little tricksters. So how do you outfox the little buggers? Following are some of the techniques we use. You can also find a large number of hits on the Internet on a search for "pilling cats" that offer helpful advice on various approaches.

Our techniques are based on years of experience in getting pills into cats. We have ranked the methods in order of ease of application and conservation of time. We have found that when four or five cats in the inn require medication, orally pilling cats can slow things to a crawl, so we avoid it whenever we can.

GRINDING PILLS OUT – ONE WAY OR ANOTHER

• *Splitting and Crushing* – Many pills can be crushed and mixed into a cat's wet food. Sixty to seventy percent of our cats get their medicine down in this manner. A few will consume a whole pill (if it is fairly small) when it is buried in the wet food. They are voracious enough eaters so they don't notice the pill. We also tuck the pill down into the wet food at times, then place two or three treats on top of the pill. This makes it hard for kitty to tell the difference between a crunching pill or crunching treat.

For crushing, we use a regular pill splitter/crusher available at most local drugstores. I put a little wet food into the coated paper food tray we use and then sprinkle the crushed pill over the surface. The next step is to lay a fresh layer of food on top of the already medicated portion to mask the presence of the medicine. This works for most cats and medicines. Another method is to use a wet food that has a lot of gravy. Most cats love the gravy and seem to be more forgiving of the presence of foreign substances if the gravy level is high. If the cat won't eat the pill in his regular food, we'll change up his diet a bit and give him something different – like a fish product with lots of gravy. Fish has a strong smell and taste and overcomes objections to the presence of the medicine with many of our boarders.

• *Pill in Your Desert* – Some cats will eat their pill in a pill-pocket. Some will not. Some will eat the pill-pocket and mouth the pill right out on the floor. As soon as they hit the crunch in the middle of the soft pill pocket they know it's time to hit the eject button. To get around this, I take the pill-pocket, place the pill in it, then take three crunchy cat treats and press them around the sides of the soft pill pocket. If the cat likes treats, and most do like one flavor or another of these little "candies," they can't seem to tell the difference between the crunching of the "candy" and that of the pill. Since they get the crunch of the treat from the start, they do not seem to know where the crunchy treat stops and the pill starts.

• *Dissolving in Water* – One cat we board is a complete Houdini, that can spit out a pill in more ways than any other cat we have ever met. She also will not eat any wet food that has been adulterated with medicine of any kind. One sniff of such a dish and she turns up her nose and walks away. So now we have to step up our game. Thus the "dissolve the pill" technique.

Originally, I crushed the pill then poured a bit of water into the crusher cylinder and let the pill thoroughly dissolve. At that point I would suck the mixture of water and medicine up with a soft nosed syringe (one similar to what is used to give children liquid medicine). Prying the cats mouth open just a bit, you can insert the syringe in between the canine teeth and far enough back to deliver the mixture. Since the syringe cylinder is round and fairly small it slips in between the cat's canine teeth fairly easily. It also prevents the cat from being able to bite down on my finger, etc., making it safer for me. My wife then simplified the whole procedure by pulling the plunger part of the syringe out of the body and dropping the pill in. She would then pour a bit of water into the cylinder, reinsert the plunger and wait for the pill to dissolve before medicating the cat. Although it might take 10 minutes or so for the pill to dissolve, you can be doing other things in the meantime. The "syringe" technique has worked well for us and is also somewhat of a time-saver.

• *Manual Pilling* – There is a ton of advice on the Internet complete with videos and all on manually pilling cats and they can provide you with a good education on the subject.

• *Stick It In Your Ear* – There are some medicines that can be topically delivered these days. Thyroid ointment is one of them. Most of us are familiar with the topical medicines used for flea treatment. There are products for treating for worms and antibiotic products for wounds, infections etc. We always make sure to use a plastic glove to apply medications so we are not absorbing the medicine ourselves. One of our customers had some bad thyroid test results recently and the doctors could not understand what was going on until they found out he was applying a topical thyroid medicine to his kitty's ear with his bare finger. Once he started wearing a glove his distorted thyroid problem disappeared.

• *Insulin shots* – One of our customers that was a nurse trained us in giving insulin shots to her cat so we could continue to board him after he became diabetic (see Sugar Daddy story). It was not as difficult as we imagined it would be to give the shots. Some cats are more problematic to give the shot to at the Inn because they are not familiar with us or the environment. The presence of the other cats also contributes to the diabetic cats discomfort level. Even when cats are at the vets they are usually the only cat in an exam room and so are more manageable. A local vet tech or your own veterinarian can teach you the mechanics of giving the shot. Most will help you as they realize you will, at some point, be boarding one of their diabetic patients. We always try to make sure that both my wife and I are around when we have to give the shots, as I hold the cat while my wife administers the injection.

• *Hydration* – We have hydrated a few cats in our time, but it is a procedure we do not like to perform. If you are a vet tech or medical professional of some type, you will probably be comfortable with the process. Hydration involves inserting a needle under the cat's skin that is connected to a saline solution bag (just like an IV). The fluid is allowed to flow till the proper amount has been administered. Cats with kidney problems can suffer from severe dehydration, and no matter how much water they drink they still become dehydrated. Some cats will get a treatment every day and others will get one every other day or so. This is a medically intensive procedure as far as I'm concerned and I don't like doing it, although I frequently get talked into it by a customer who pleads with us to do it. Another solution is to hire a local vet tech to come in and treat the cat as opposed to doing it yourself, especially in your first few years.

A FINAL WORD ON MEDICATIONS

Keep in mind that cat owners with cats on meds are a very important prospective customer group for any cat boarding business. The only way the owner can be sure kitty gets its meds is by boarding it. At home, the cat can easily run and hide from a pet sitter, family member or whoever is trying to care for them. In a boarding facility they have nowhere to hide, so they are going to get their medicine one way or another. Make sure all your marketing promotion materials, web site etc., mention that you administer meds. It will be important to your success.

CHAPTER 16

DEALING WITH SCARY CATS

For the most part life in the B&B is peaceful, and a majority of the cats are just nice "little people in fur coats." It's the ones that do not fit that profile that can make life exciting, sometimes stimulating beyond your wildest dreams. Your first extremely aggressive cat will be an experience you won't readily forget. I have found there are two types of aggressive cat situations. The first is what I would call "temporary situational based" and the second is "long term personality based."

When cats arrive at the inn (especially those unfamiliar with your facility or cats being boarded for the first time) they are apt to be upset. Even kitties that are totally peaceful at home can display some aggression when they first arrive at the inn. Look at it from their point of view. The surroundings are unfamiliar, they smell all the other cats and feel trapped in their carrier with numerous potential threats surrounding them.

Under these circumstances, even a mild mannered cat is likely to display some hissing and spitting behavior. This is completely normal. We never push them at this point or force ourselves on them. They will scratch or worse.

Some cats are truly aggressive. They are not friendly, will attack, and usually don't mellow much with age. We have to be constantly on guard with such cats because they can and will hurt us if we get careless.

Most cats we board that act aggressively do so because of fear.

They're in a strange place with a lot of strange cats. They feel cornered with no place to run. And last, but not least, they have no idea what this strange person hanging around (that's me) is up to. With most of these cats a little understanding goes a long way. You also may find it hard to believe, but the cat that wants to tear you to pieces today may be your good buddy given a day or so to adjust to his new situation. The trick is to stay calm, talk soothingly, avoid fast movements, and don't look at the cat directly in the eyes as long as he/she is upset. Direct eye contact is threatening. When a cat that has been acting out comes out of his bed or carrier and meows at you, the corner has been turned. Things will start improving. That first tentative meow almost always means,

"I'm ready to be your friend now."

But we don't let our guard down too quickly.

I thought it might be helpful to describe how we deal with some specific cats. Each cat is unique, and the stories will help you see how we interact with cats that are displaying some type of aggressive behavior. Also keep in mind that the word "aggressive" (especially when you find a vet using the term) tends to be reserved for cats that will have no hesitation about attacking you. Some short term bad behavior does not mean a cat is truly aggressive in the sense it will continue to be a danger to those caring for it.

• *Juliane* – Juliane is a beautiful orange tabby that has arrived at the inn ready to do battle (as though her life is in imminent danger) for the past seven years. Every time she comes we go through the same process. Her dad brings in her bed and other accouterments which we get all set up in her condo. Then, when given the all clear signal, mom exits the car carrying Juliane, who melts like butter in mom's arms with a hypnotic, far-away look of peace and tranquility on her face. Mom approaches the condo and places Juliane on the floor, where, depending on her mood-of-the-day, all hell can break loose. She'll hiss, spit, and make fake charges at me, even whacking at the door of the condo in an attempt to reach me. After her parents leave she will go up to the sleeping shelf and climb into her bed, pausing at appropriate intervals to peek over the top of the bed and tell me what she thinks of me in no uncertain terms (I have learned to understand "felineese"). If I reach into the condo in front of her in the first couple of days of her visit she will whack me real good with her paw. So, how do you open her condo door, get her litter box out, clean the unit and feed her? Good question.

I have found that Juliane, as with most cats, has respect for one thing in the cat room – the hissing head of the vacuum cleaner. When she sees me approaching her unit with the vacuum wand, she will quickly run up to the top shelf and watch intently as I vacuum and clean her unit. As long as I keep my head lower than her position on the top shelf, and do not make direct eye contact, she will let me do everything that has to be done. She waits for me to finish up, signaled by the arrival of her new plate of food and water, and as soon as I exit and clip the door she comes down and starts eating. Juliane loosens up quite a bit after three or four days. She will come to the condo door and rub around as if saying, "I'd like a little bit of rubbing." I can reach through with my finger and stroke her briefly, at which point she is liable to spin around and try to get me. I have learned to be very quick getting my finger out of there. I think this is all some sort of game with her, and I have learned to enjoy her unique personality and deal with her in a way that works for both of us. Juliane has taught me how to be a loving innkeeper even when the going gets tough. You can learn something from almost every kitty that comes to stay with you.

• *Miss Tish* – Miss Tish is a delicate little torti with an elephantine sized attitude. When she arrives I place the carrier with her in it in her condo. The minute she can see me through the screen mesh door of the carrier she lets out with what could best be described as a convulsive hissy fit. My gosh, can that little creature make a horrible, really scary bunch of noises. She tries repeatedly to attack my hand through the screen on her soft sided carrier as I try to get a grip on the zipper to open it. I learned the hard way she can get a claw through that screen and into me.

My current technique for dealing with her involves putting on my Kevlar gloves then rubbing one finger over the surface of the door screen. She focuses on and attacks the moving glove as I surreptitiously unzip the screen with the other hand. Believe me, once unzipped, I get both of my hands out of there fast, shut the condo door and give her some time to cool off. Oila! Job safely accomplished.

For the next day or so, Miss Tish will reside in the carrier and leap forward to try to attack anything that enters or even gets too close in front of her condo door. This always goes on for about a day or so after her arrival. By the third day she will come out of her carrier when she sees me come into the cat room and let out a somewhat strident meow, a hint that she is considering acting in a civilized manner if I feed her what she wants. At that point all is forgiven and life returns to normal. I do keep my hands out of her way for another day or so though, as from time to time she will decide that I need additional schooling in appropriate behavior.

Even at their calmest, I still exercise care with cats like Miss Tish. Each cat has to be treated in a way that accommodates their individual foibles. Some of my visitors look fearful, but they will let me pat them and give them a rubbing with no problem at all. Others fall all along the trend line that goes from the calmest to the Miss Tish level.

I still do have to use the vacuum trick with Miss Tish though, because you never quite know when she is going to get on her "high horse" about something. She is one of those kitties that finds the hissing vac fascinating, and will jump up on her shelf and observe the whole cleaning process as if it is a pretty cool event.

Actually, I have gotten quite fond of Miss Tish on her numerous visits, and have enjoyed the challenge of making friends with her. But the hair on the back of my neck still goes up the day she arrives and issues her first few blood-chilling screams.

• *Vinnie the Mobster* – Vinnie is a huge twenty-plus pound orange tabby cat that I am sure has a feline gangland background. If cats toted tommy guns, that would be Vinnie. Just the way he looks at you is scary. He still intimidates me for a few days after his arrival, even though he has been coming now for at least five or so years. He also strikes fear into the other cats. None wander too close past his door more than once.

Vinnie is another one of those cats that goes into his unit in his carrier. Getting the carrier placed in the unit is not a problem but then the fun starts. We now have to open the carrier door and Vinnie will not permit anybody to get a hand within a foot without going into attack mode. Unfortunately, the carrier door has holes big enough for Vinnie to get his claws through and get you, so, like with Miss Tish, you have to develop a technique that will allow the door to be safely opened. To make it even more fun, the slide catch on Vinnie's carrier is extremely difficult to grasp and slide. Trying it with bare hands is suicide.

I have a small, thin Teflon cutting board in the office to use for this task, but any thin material, like a cookie sheet, etc. would work. I slide the cutting board over the screened surface of the carrier door right up against the slide catch, effectively blocking Vinnie from getting his claws through the door. I can then operate the catch, releasing the door to permit Vinnie's exit. Vinnie also presents a problem when it is time to clean his unit. He sits by the condo door and almost dares me to enter his lair.

"Bring it on, baby. I'm ready."

Once again the business end of the hissing vacuum saves the day. Vinnie will bat the wand a few times, but then he gets annoyed and goes into his carrier. A push on the carrier door with the wand closes the door and then we reverse the carrier door opening procedure previously described. After cleaning, we repeat the process again and Vinnie is ready for another day at the inn.

• *Charley* – Charley was a she – a slim little cat that moved with lightening speed. She had a voice that could freeze people in their tracks. There were countless times that Charley scared the living daylights out of me with her histrionics. Most of this behavior was prompted by fear, I am sure, but could this little kitty put on a show. No one visiting the cat room would go near her once they heard her blood curdling scream, a noise that literally would make your hair stand on end and send a chill down your spine. Couple that with her unbelievably energetic fits of hissing and spitting and you can understand why Charley did not readily make friends. I had to be careful with Charley, but once you understood what made her tick she became quite manageable. If you accept all of these kitties as a challenge to overcome, life will be a lot more fun.

Charley loved one particular unit in our boarding area that we call the Tower Unit. It is a fairly narrow vertical unit designed to fit right next to the picture window. Charley would sit on the top shelf and watch everything that happened outside. Passersby on the sidewalk and workers in the cranberry bogs across the street were subjected to the closest scrutiny.

When I was cleaning, Charley would jump down to the middle shelf of the unit which guaranteed that I could not reach any part of it without her permission. I started holding the paper towel roll between Charley and my face while I cleaned. Charley would whale away at the roll with her front paws, actually knocking it out of my hands more than a few times, but she never hurt me. It all seemed to be a big game. A couple of times when she succeeded in knocking the roll out of my hands, she beat a steady tattoo on my head, but once again, she never hurt me. In one of those overenthusiastic bursts of energy she managed to swipe the glasses off my face with those lightening fast paws of hers but left nary a scratch. And whenever I came up to face to face level and looked her directly, eye-to-eye, she would break into a hissing spitting fit just inches from my face, but by that time I had learned what I could get away with and what I could not. But bless her little heart, she never did hurt me or attempt to bite.

Charley's owners had a son, John, that Charley absolutely hated. No one had a clue as to as to why. While on vacation in Plymouth,

John came by one day to pick up Charley for his mom and dad. As he walked into the cat room he said,

"Watch this."

Charley went absolutely nuts the minute she spotted John. I had never heard the likes of the show that Charley put on that day, although we did get to see a repeat performance under somewhat unusual circumstances.

On that particular day, Dave, Charley's owner had come to pick up Charley and my son Jack happened to be visiting. Dave looked at Jack and commented,

"Wow, you look so much like my son it is amazing."

A twinkle came into his eye as he said to my son,

"Why don't you come on in and meet my cat Charley."

Like a lamb led to the slaughter Jack walked into the room with Dave. As they walked up to Charley's condo Charley took one look at Jack and exploded into that same awesome repertoire of hers. My son, expecting to meet a calm little pussy cat, jumped backwards in horror, totally unprepared for anything like the show that Charley was putting on. Jack's interest in extending his visit with Charley immediately evaporated while Dave howled with laughter at Charley's reaction.

Not too long ago I received an email from Dave, as he and Sue had moved to Virginia. Poor Charley had become gravely ill and passed away. I was struck with sadness as I reflected on my memories of that feisty little cat and the adventures we had together. Charley will always be remembered at the Inn with the greatest of affection.

• *Minty* – Minty's first stay with us started innocuously enough. When the doorbell rang, I opened the door to be greeted by an impeccably dressed lady with a cat carrier in one hand and a white box wrapped with red ribbon in the other. Once Deb was in the office she expressed her gratitude for our being available to take care of Minty while she was away and gave us the white box, which contained an impressive assortment of excellent quality chocolates. I remember thinking to myself at the time what a thoughtful thing it was for her to do. A short time later I realized this gift was an apology in advance for the behavior of what turned out to be, arguably, the most hostile little kitty we have ever boarded.

We have boarded thousands of cats over the last umpteen years, and we have probably only had five to ten that exhibited the level of intensity Minty presented. But you should be prepared when you finally do have a "Minty" visit with you. We tell the story in detail because the techniques I had to use were necessary to keep myself safe from Minty's extreme behavior.

Minty was doing a whole lot of hissing and spitting, but when we got close to the carrier, she started to make a "kaaking" sound, a sound I have learned to treat with great respect. This sound explodes from deep within the cat's throat and has a somewhat gutteral quality. It can be accompanied by laid back ears, crouched body and wide open mouth with teeth bared. Many such cats will also make a series of feinting moves, as if they are going to lunge at you. Believe me, they will attack if you push them.

I placed Minty's carrier on the bottom shelf one of our upper level studio units. This places the cat at about the same level as my face. Minty was making ferocious noises and whacking at her owners hands while she was trying to unlatch the carrier door. Once the door popped loose, Deb quickly withdrew her hands. After a few pleasantries, she was on her way.

Feeling safe from Minty's wrath at that point, I wandered over to get a better look at the kitty. She exploded out of the carrier springing onto the condo's door, hissing, spitting and "kaacking" a continuous stream of unearthly sounding feline epithets. What a gosh awful assortment of sounds that cat could make. For the remainder of the day anytime I came near the condo she would lunge out of her carrier trying to get at me through the door. It was going to be a real chore trying to care for this cat without one of us suffering bodily harm. That first night I was barely able to slip a dish of wet food through the cracked open condo door so she could eat. I was dreading the next morning when I would have to clean Minty's unit. How in the heck was I going to be able to manage that challenge? True to form, the next morning Minty resumed attack mode the minute I came near her door. There was no way I was going to get my hands in that unit without her getting a piece of me. I had to figure out some way to manage the situation.

Starting the vac and approaching her unit with the hissing wand, I cracked the door open and inserted it into the unit. Minty attacked the end of the vac a couple of times but then decided she would not rather deal with it and went into her carrier. I tried to reach in and close the carrier door, but the advance of my hands resulted in another charge from the carrier and my quick retreat. The challenge would be to get her closed in that carrier without putting my hands in the unit.

Luckily, we have screened doors in our units. We used the screen doors on our condos because we felt that it would offer better air circulation and not seal the cats behind a sheet of plexi, creating a rather sterile, unfriendly environment. The mesh on the screen is about one inch by two inches, allowing me to insert a narrow strip of wood (or dowel) through the screen. I pushed the wood strip through the screen and used it to shove the carrier door shut. Now I was able to keep the pressure on the carrier door while I slipped my hand (with protective glove) into the unit and clipped the carrier door. It required a bit of dexterity, but it worked. After cleaning the unit and providing fresh water and food all I had to do was use the glove, unclip the door and get "out of town" real quick. Usually she was in hot pursuit of my gloved hand, but we were making it work and it looked like Minty would be able to survive her stay – and me too!

As time went on she began to forsake the carrier and stay on the top shelf when I had to clean. This left me exposed, but by that time if I just held the vacuum up between my face and hers she would stay on the shelf and let me work. If she became testy, sometimes I would have to use one of those "grabbers" with the clamps on the end to grip the food dishes without exposing my hands and arms. A gift for problem solving and coming up with "outside the box" solutions, I have found, is an indispensable tool for an innkeeper to have in his/her arsenal of weapons.

Minty visited a number of times and we were able to deal with her by being creative in our approach. And Minty did teach us another valuable lesson – beware of customers who bring boxes of chocolates with them when they come to drop off their cats.

• *Gretzel* – Gretzel is the only other cat we have boarded that was in the same league as Minty. Actually the adjective "aggressive"- does not do Gretzel justice. Calling her a feline psychopath would be a compliment. Gretzel was truly vicious and attacked anything and anyone that came near her – except for her mistress, Lynn. She was the only person that could get near the cat, and her husband was not accorded the same respect. He finally banned her from the house when she took to urinating on his side of the bed – not Lynn's mind you, just his. Who says cats don't know what they are doing.

Lynn searched and searched, but could not find any one or even a shelter that would take Gretzel. Since Lynn was under orders to have the cat put down if no other solution could be found, she decided to board Gretzel with us until she found a way out of her dilemma. Unfortunately, we were not aware of the full scope of the situation we were getting involved in before Gretzel arrived. Gretzel, we were told, was very unfriendly, but that had to be one of the great understatements of all time. We began to suspect that we were in trouble when we met Gretzel for the first time and observed her psychotic behavior. Lynn paid us in cash for the first two weeks and told us she would be traveling and would come by at the end of her trip. She told us to never call her at home for any reason, only on her cell phone and never in the evening. It seems that Lynn's husband was under the impression that she had complied with his wishes and that Gretzel had already been dispatched to the happy hunting grounds for cats. It was crucial that we not let the "cat out of the bag" and reveal that Gretzel was still in the land of the living.

It only took a few days for us to fully understand that there was no way this cat could ever be adopted. There was absolutely no sign of improvement in her behavior. We had to wear Kevlar gloves to put her food dishes in her condo, and she attacked every time we fed her.

After about a month of paying us in cash and sneaking down to see us and say hello to Gretzel, Lynn realized there was no hope. She would have to put Gretzel to sleep, and in spite of the cat's behavior, she was distraught. Empathizing with the pain she was in and how difficult it would be to follow through, I told her to make the arrangements with her vet and I would take Gretzel for the appointment.

It was a sad ending for a rather handsome calico cat that would have made a beautiful pet if only it could have behaved in a reasonable manner. As we tell many of the foster children that have lived with us over the years, choices have consequences. Make good choices because we all have to live with the results of our choices. Bad choices lead to bad endings.

CHAPTER 17

APPENDIX

If you would like to be notified when the
Pampered Cats Cat Boarding Manual is published,
visit www.josephgarvey.com and subscribe to email newsletter.

Introducing the Cat Boarding Alternative You've Dreamed of But Could Never Find.

See us on the web at
www.pamperedcats.com

A luxury Bed & Breakfast Inn for Felines
in Plymouth, MA

Mailing address: P. O. Box 1016, Manomet, MA 02345
126 Manomet Point Road, Manomet, MA
508-224-7085

Hosts: Joe & Carol Garvey

Figure 1 – Cover of 8.5 x 11 promotional sales brochure –folds to 3.75" x 8.75"

Pampered Cats is a first class
Bed & Breakfast exclusively for cats.

FOUR PAW RATED

- Specializing in long and short-term boarding.
- Homey, warm and loving environment.
- Your pet is personally cared for by the owners.
- Owners in residence so your kitty is never alone overnight.
- Our prime concerns are that your kitty is kept safe, healthy, well entertained and socialized.
- Spacious condos measure approximately 3 x 4 x 8 high. Studio units meet the special needs of the elderly, heavy and timid cats and kittens.
- Plenty of room in these multi-level condos for a favorite blanket or toys from home to make your kitty comfortable.
- Individual and family accommodations.
- Super-suite unit available for a large family or cat with special needs.
- Every cat has a panoramic outdoor view.
- Each cat has its own afghan, toys and daily socialization.
- Premium foods (or we serve your own) and large litter boxes.
- Special diets catered to.

- If your cat needs medical attention while you're away, we'll take it to your own veterinarian if at all possible.
- Climate control includes heating and air conditioning.
- Latest materials and techniques used to assure unmatched cleanliness.
- Private playtime provided for all kitties.
- Competitive rates.
- Pre-boarding inspection is welcome. Call for appointment.

FOUR PAW RATED

For the well-being of all our guests, documentation of current rabies and feline distemper inoculations within the year is required before we can board your cat. Male animals must be neutered.

FOUR PAW RATED

Studio units & condos overlook scenic cranberry bog.

Phone at left shows full size condo.

Figure 2 – Interior of promotional sales brochure - 8.5 x 11 inches

Luxury Boarding for Cats

Pampered Cats

126 Manomet Point Road
Plymouth, MA
Mail: P. O. Box 1016
Manomet, MA 02345
Tel. 508-224-7085

Web & Email
www.pamperedcats.com
joecarol@ pamperedcats.com

Owners
Joe & Carol Garvey

Figure 3 – Business card

Pampered Cats

Date In ____/____/____/_____   Date Out____/____/____/_____
     Mo.   Date Day Wk. Time   Mo. Day   Day Wk. Time

Name_____

Telephone #   Home_____Work_____

Cell _____ _____ _____   Emergency _____ _____ _____

*EMAIL ADDRESS*_____

Instructions/Food/Cat Info:_____

Medical Instructions_____

Flea Treatment ?_____

Veterinarian_____   *Invoice Calculation*

Date Reservation Made_____/_____/_____
                    Mo.   Date

Name_____Age____Sex____Alt.____Desc._____

Name_____Age____Sex____Alt.____Desc._____

Name_____Age____Sex____Alt.____Desc._____

Name_____Age____Sex____Alt.____Desc._____   **2015**

January	February	March	April	May	June

July	August	September	October	November	December

Regular Rates ••• 1 cat--$17.00; 2 cats --$25.00; 3 cats--$30.00; 4 cats--$35.00; 5 cats--$42.00
Long Term/Indefinite Stays -- Monthly payments in advance.
Medications – $1.50 per application • **Insulin** – $2.00 per shot.• **Hydration** – $15.00 per

Figure 4 – Reservation Sheet

Pampered Cats
A luxury Bed & Breakfast Inn for Felines
in Plymouth, MA

126 Manomet Point Road, Manomet, MA 02345
Mailing Address: P. O. Box 1016, Manomet, MA 02345 • 508-224-7085

FOR IMMEDIATE RELEASE

For more information contact:
Carol or Joe Garvey
P. O. Box 1016, Manomet, MA 02345

MANOMET COUPLE OPENS AREA'S
FIRST CAT HOUSE.

When Joe & Carol Garvey decided to go away to Maine for a long weekend, they never dreamed a chain of events was being unleashed that would result in the establishment of a luxury "Bed & Breakfast" for cats.

"For years we had college age and working children around to care for our cats when we went away", says Carol. "But our children are all grown and married now. So off we went to tour cat boarding kennels. That s when we began to realize that finding our pampered kitties a place just like home was not going to be easy."

"The cages at many of the places we visited were just too small. Frequently dogs were located near and sometimes right across the isle from the cats. I knew my cats were going to be totally stressed out."

"One day during our search I happened to open Yankee Magazine and saw an article on a lady operating a cats-only boarding cattery out of her home in Maine. Each cat had a spacious enclosure. The enclosures were big enough to house several cats from the same family. Each condo, as she called them, had a couple of sleeping shelves, cushions, toys and really BIG litter boxes. Because the service was run out of her home, the animals were never left alone for hours at a time or overnight. The cats enjoyed premium food, had windows to look out, spent time outside their enclosure and were given daily socialization time and brushing. The owner called her kennel a "Bed and Breakfast for Cats". After a tour, we found ourselves wishing there was a facility like it closer to our home."

"At that point, everything sort of jelled. We knew there was a need because there must be other people like us looking for a really special place to board their cat. Our big old empty nest home had a wing

-- more --

Figure 5 – News Release sent to media – Page 1

Appendix

that would be perfect for the task. That s how Pampered Cats came into being."

"The whole purpose of Pampered Cats is to offer all the amenities and services cat lovers seek. Our goal is to provide for the safety and health of each guest in a warm, spacious and homey environment. We provide loving personal care, the best in food, spring water, an afghan and pillow for each kitty. We cater to special diets, welcome kitty s favorite toys, and have enough room for a sweater their owner wears, for example, or a special blanket from home. Basically, whatever it takes to make kitty comfortable. If the sound of your voice soothes your pet just leave us a tape and we ll play it for him or her. We believe in doing everything we can to make your pet comfortable and treat each animal like it was our own."

"The condos at Pampered Cats are about 3 foot by 4 foot by 8 foot and have three separate levels so kitties have plenty of room to move around. We also have a few studio units that are a bit smaller (3 x4 x4) but are competitively priced with the much smaller cages available in most kennels."

"Cats are occupied with entertainment in the form of soft music with birds singing and nature videos that are a kitties wildest fantasy. Everybody is allowed free time out of their condo every day to roam around, play, look out the windows, check out the birds and say hello to their neighbors. Each kitty also has toys that it can physically play with to satisfy its need to "bat" things around."

"Since the condos are located in a wing of our home, your kitty is ensured of the maximum possible attention and is never left alone in an unoccupied building over night. Or worse, left unattended during a bad storm. At Pampered Cats, we re almost always here. Lots of times we go into the cattery to catch up on our reading just to provide our guests with additional company. Before going to bed we also check in with our guests to make sure everything is OK and say goodnight . I feel better when I know all my kitties are doing fine. That s what Pampered Cats is all about."

-- 30 --

Figure 5 – News Release sent to media – Page 2

191

Best Friends

PLYMOUTH'S 'CAT CONDO'

Pampered Cats is 'luxury feline B&B'

By Anne M. Oliver
The Patriot Ledger

The brochure reads like this: a three-story condo in scenic Plymouth with a view of the cranberry bogs and gourmet meals for only $56 a week. If this sounds too good to be true that's because it is, unless you happen to be a cat.

Pampered Cats is a "luxury bed and breakfast for felines," say its owners, Carol and Joe Garvey of Plymouth. The couple renovated a wing of their home in March to create a deluxe kennel for cats only.

There are eight condos, each 3-by-4-by-8 feet; a much larger super suite can accommodate a family of three. Each cat gets its own afghan, toys and time out of the cage each day. The Garveys groom each cat daily and serve premium foods and spring water. Carol Garvey said she prefers the Excel and Nutro brands of food available at pet specialty stores. She said she tested them with her "feline board of advisors," and they were the favorites. She will also serve food provided by the cats' owners.

The units are heated and air conditioned, and the air is filtered. If a cat has a medical problem during its stay at Pampered Cats, the Garveys say they will even take it to the vet.

The idea for a cat condo came to the couple after they had a difficult time finding a place to board their three cats while they went to Maine, said Carol Garvey, a former real estate agent and computer programmer. Their children, who used to watch the cats, had all moved out on their own. Then Garvey said she read an article in Yankee magazine about a woman who had started a cat-only boarding facility in her Maine home. The couple visited the facility and the idea was hatched.

"The cages at many of the places we visited were just too small," said Garvey. "In some places, dogs were right across the aisle from the cats.

I knew my cats would be totally stressed out.

"We almost got cold feet, but I couldn't see how it wouldn't work. I knew there must be other people out there like us."

Joe Garvey, who works in marketing and advertising, took a six-month leave to start the business. He built the kennel himself for about $4,000. Given the number of customers they have served since the opening in June, the couple may convert two additional rooms for Pampered Cats.

Several customers, such as Fran Sullivan of Quincy, say they're pleased. Sullivan was frantically trying to find a home for Meepers and Sooty when she went to Europe for eight weeks this summer.

"I looked for months, and I couldn't find anything," she said. "I was thinking of them being in these little tiny cages for eight weeks. I was thinking I might have to cancel my trip. But then I found out about Pampered Cats and it was wonderful.

"I'm telling you, these cats didn't want to come home. It may have cost a little more than I could afford, but the whole time I was in Europe I had peace of mind. I would have paid anything for that."

Pampered Cats is comparable in price to other cat boarding facilities, but the average size of the cages at most kennels is much smaller. One local kennel charges $7 per day for a cage that is 2.5-by-2.5-by-3 feet.

Before a cat can stay, its owners must show proof it has been inoculated within the past year for rabies, feline distemper and leukemia. Male cats must be neutered.

Garvey said many of the cats are upset when they first arrive, but usually calm down within 24 hours. One recent day, Penny and Bingo were the only guests at the kennel,

Haley Garvey, 3, and Joe Garvey check on cats at Pampered Cats, a deluxe kennel the family runs in Manomet.
Fred Field photos/The Patriot Ledger

and Penny spent most of the time a visitor was there rubbing against Garvey's leg and climbing on her desk. The day before Penny, a five-year-old Calico and Tortoiseshell mix, was very upset and howling when she arrived. Meanwhile, Bingo was hanging out in his condo with a pillowcase hung in front with clothespins for privacy.

"Bingo is one of those cats that doesn't really like being with other cats," Garvey said. "We hang up these privacy screens so they don't have to see the other cats if they don't want to."

Pampered Cats charges $8 per day for the first cat, $7 for the second, and $6 for the third from the same family. Joe and Carol Garvey say they are willing to accommodate special diets and will pick up and drop off cats if necessary.

Carol Garvey says Pampered Cats serves premium foods and spring water to their feline guests.

Figure 6 – Story from local newspaper resulting from news release

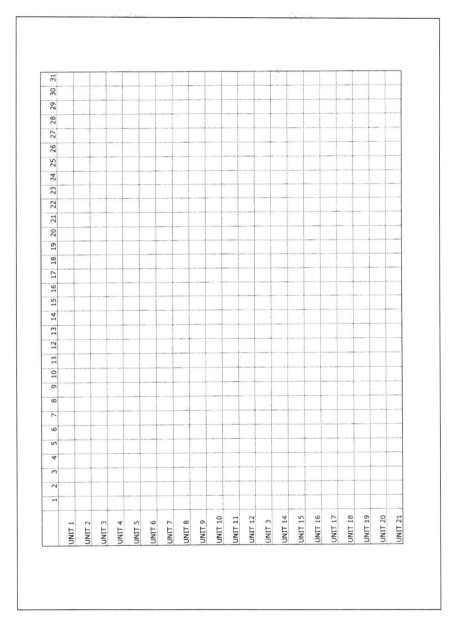

Figure 7 – Manual schedule chart for room planning.

Figure 8 – Vehicle sign

Figure 9– Lawn signage

Pampered Cats

A luxury Bed & Breakfast Inn for Felines
in Plymouth, MA
126 Manomet Point Road • Mail address: P.O. Box 1016, Manomet MA 02345 • 508-224-7085

THE PAMPERED CATS MEMORANDUM OF UNDERSTANDING

The owners of Pampered Cats of Plymouth, Carol and Joe Garvey, will take every consideration and precaution to ensure the safety, comfort and well being of your pet.

For your cat's protection, you agree to the following conditions:

1) Documentation of current rabies innoculation for all cats in addition to feline distemper shot for cats under 10 years of age.

2) We highly recommend feline leukemia testing and inoculation for cats allowed outside of their home.

3) We have your permission to take your cat to the veterinarian in case of illness, at your expense. You agree to pay such expenses at the time you pick your cat up. If your vet is unavailable at the time, we will take your pet to a vet of our choice.

4) We have your permission to treat your cat, at your expense, if he/she arrives with fleas.

5) We have your permission to treat your cat for hairballs, earmites or tapeworms when those conditions are present, at your expense, if we feel it is necessary.

6) Male cats must be neutered.

7) If your cat is left at Pampered Cats for a period of more than one week beyond the date below specified as "Pick up date", without an adjustment to this contract in writing, that Pampered Cats has the right to place the cat in an adoptive home, or, if that is not possible, we have the right to resolve the situation as we deem necessary.

The boarding/grooming fee agreed on is payable in advance on weekly basis.

We sincerely appreciate the trust you have shown in us by boarding your companion here. We treat every pet as if it were our own!

Pick up date_____

Pet Owner's Signature_____ Date ___ ___ ___

Pampered Cats Signature _____ Date ___ ___ ___

Curent Rates: 1 Cat: $15.00 per day 2 Cats: $23.00 per day 3 Cats: $28.00 per day 4 Cats: $32.00 per day
          5 Cats: $37.00 per day

Figure 10 – Contract shown only for information purposes.
You should obtain approval from legal counsel on your contract.

INDEX